Life!

Celebrate It

The Alchemy of the Heart

I Married Adventure

Notes to a Working Woman

Wide My World, Narrow My Bed

You Bring the Confetti, God Brings the Joy

Life!

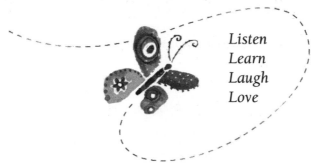

Listen
Learn
Laugh
Love

Celebrate It

luci swindoll

W PUBLISHING GROUP
A Division of Thomas Nelson Publishers
Since 1798

www.wpublishinggroup.com

LIFE! CELEBRATE IT

Published by W Publishing Group, a division of Thomas Nelson, Inc., P.O. Box 141000, Nashville, TN 37214.

W Publishing Group books may be purchased in bulk for educational, business, fundraising, or sales promotional use. For information, please email SpecialMarkets@ThomasNelson.com.

All Scripture quotations, unless otherwise indicated, are taken from The New King James Version, © 1984 by Thomas Nelson, Inc. Other Scripture quotations are taken from the following: The King James Version of the Bible (KJV). Public domain. *The Message* by Eugene H. Peterson (MSG), copyright © 1993, 1994, 1995, 1996, 2000, 2001, 2002. Used by permission of NavPress Publishing Group. All rights reserved. The Holy Bible, New International Version © (NIV®). Copyright © 1973, 1978, 1984 by International Bible Society. Used by permission of Zondervan. All rights reserved. The Living Bible (TLB). Copyright © 1971 by Tyndale House Publishers, Inc. Used by permission. All rights reserved.

Cover design: Studio Olika, Cincinnati, Ohio

Library of Congress Cataloging-in-Publication Data
Swindoll, Luci, 1932–
  Life: celebrate it! / Luci Swindoll.
    p. cm.
  Summary: "Answers to questions about balancing life and a quality life that is very full"—Provided by publisher.
  Includes bibliographical references.

  ISBN 0-8499-0051-4 (hardcover)

  1. Christian life.   I. Title.
BV4501.3.S96   2006
248.4—dc22   2005033073

Printed in the United States of America
06 07 08 09 10 QW 9 8 7 6 5 4 3

*This book is affectionately dedicated with appreciation
to my wonderful friends:*

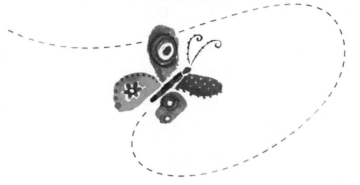

SANDY LOUGH

AND

RUTH CRONIN-FRUITT

*Together we have celebrated life to the fullest for thirty years,
listening, learning, laughing, and loving.*

What joy they have brought to my heart!

Contents

Foreword

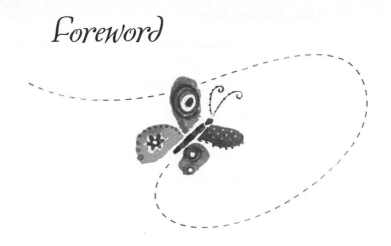

Luci Swindoll has been my friend and almost constant companion on the road for many years. I've traveled literally all over the world with her—she's searched for adventure and I for a nice rest. (How we've managed to find both without driving one another crazy is another story.)

I'm actually a good traveler with a lot of experience. I learned to travel in my years with Campus Crusade for Christ, and by the time I met Luci in the late seventies, I knew how to get almost anywhere in the world without fear or intimidation, with no second language, and very little money. I often scared my parents but never myself. I knew how to travel long before I met Luci.

What I didn't know, frankly, was how to live. I went everywhere, but sights and sounds flew by me without my even paying attention. When Luci and I started traveling here and there together, I could get us anywhere in the world on a shoestring. But when we arrived? That's when Luci took over.

You see, Luci knows not only how to live but how to live well. She knows how to savor life and celebrate it. She knows how to make the most of every second and live the life out of it. She knows how to listen, learn, laugh, and love. She simply knows how to live.

That's why, in thirty years' of friendship with her, I've begged her to sit with almost everyone I've ever known and talk with them about life. I ask her questions, and her answers stimulate life-changing conversations.

Is it any surprise that I now have about three million new friends through my work with Women of Faith? And I want Luci to tell them all about life and how to squeeze it for all it's worth! That's what this book does. I recommend your reading it and then passing it on to your closest three million friends.

Mary Graham
President, Women of Faith

Backward

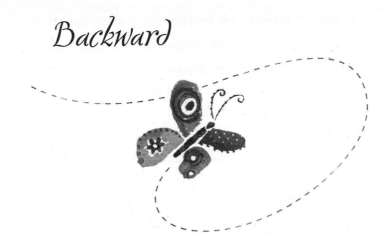

A few months ago, I saw something that intrigued me. It was a cabin cruiser in the harbor with *My First Boat* printed across the stern. "There's nothing very intriguing about that," you may say . . . but the way those words read caught my attention. Each one was printed upside down. The very smug-looking owner (admiring his work from the deck) had just finished painting the last letter. Of course, leaning over the water and looking down, he could read everything perfectly.

I laughed out loud, thinking, *How clever!* I don't know if he did it just for fun or if he really thought we could see it right side up. But either way, I loved it because it made me reflect on how often my own boat has felt upside down.

Driving along that day, I thought about my "first boat"—
the skiff that took me to the shore of my dreams and
dropped me off as an inexperienced ingenue in the days
before I knew better or had a reliable map to guide me.
With nothing more than a college degree and heart full of
anticipation, I was floating along as a complete greenhorn,
trying to get sea legs.

In our youth, we think we can do anything and go anywhere. We head out to conquer new territory across the
vast ocean of life, full of excitement, ambition, imagination,
and ignorance. At least, that was my thinking. With the
encouragement of my parents and my own personal aspirations, I hoped to find the sunken chest of life's treasures.

In my twenties, I thought I knew everything there was
to know about life. I fantasized circumstances where others
would engage me in fascinating, enriching conversation
including questions about life and how to solve its problems. I pictured open forums where I'd be seated before an
audience of my peers, hands up all over the place wanting
me to clear away the fog of their quandaries. Yeah, right.

Funny thing was, nobody asked me anything when I was
young. Nobody cared what I thought. Nobody wanted problems solved by someone who barely knew how to raise a sail.
It's hard on our ego to face the fact we know very little and

our paper-thin values do nothing but flap in the breeze. But that's the way it was. And it's even harder to realize we don't learn life's most important lessons until our boat has completely capsized and we've been forced to swim fast or tread water in an angry ocean.

And you want to know what's even more disconcerting? Now that I'm in my seventies, with gray hair and brittle bones, people ask me questions *all the time* about how I've learned to stay afloat. They want to know the secret of being a happy single woman, how I survived in the corporate world, when I planned my career, and where I learned to balance time, energy, and money. They wonder what's helped me the most as a Christian or how I experience the fullness of life. They ask about process, development, purpose, wisdom, passion, and lessons learned. All sorts of questions. Of course, they're looking for answers to their own dilemmas, just as I did when I was their age.

But I don't want to tell people how to solve their problems. I don't know enough. When I'm ninety, I still won't know enough! All I can do is take out my very marked-up map and point them in the direction of probabilities that lead to some degree of understanding and acceptance of themselves.

So that's what this book is about. It's a backward glance over seven decades of trying to figure things out so my little boat won't turn over. I've divided this book into four parts, which correlate to the four phases of life through which we all progress—listening, learning, laughing, and loving.

In my younger years, I wish I had spent less time waiting for someone to ask me for answers and more time being willing to *listen* to those who had lived long enough to actually know some of the answers. If I had listened more, then I surely would have *learned* more—about life, about others, and about myself. And as I learned from others by really listening to them, then I would have been able to *laugh* more, because let's face it: funny stuff happens in life. Although I didn't listen or learn nearly enough in my younger years, I did learn to laugh. And as I stepped back to laugh at life and myself and situations, I was finally able to fully and freely *love*—to love God, to love who He created me to be, and to love all the people God has sent to enrich my life.

If God gives you a long life, one day you'll be my age (or perhaps you are now). You'll then take time to look backward too. Your brain will simply ponder the past whether you want it to or not.

You'll have regrets and disappointments. You'll remembers sorrows you bore and temptations you failed to overcome. You'll smile when you consider joyful adventures and risks that catapulted you into achievement. You might even find tears welling up because of a loved one lost along the way or a dream that never materialized. You'll feel grateful for the fact God never let you down and for His severe mercy that taught you lessons you could have never learned unless your heart was broken.

All of that is life.

Several years ago, a dear friend gave me a thin, colorful little book called *The Atlas of Experience*.[1] It's based on the theory that human beings have always been haunted by fundamental questions and searching for answers. This book opens before the reader a sea of possibilities on which we all travel. By means of its evocative maps and routes, one can follow many passageways that lead to shorelines where our imagination, ideas, feelings, experience, and faith are enlarged. Questions may not be answered to our satisfaction, but we're made to think.

That's the way life works. It's uncertain and has myriad ups and downs. If we cannot or do not learn from these uncertainties, we'll repeat patterns that keep us treading water. And if we get stuck there, how will we find our sea legs? How will we become adults?

As long as we are in the human condition, we'll have questions. You can count on it! A few of our questions will be simple and have easy answers. Others will be difficult, taking time to work out. Some will demand processing with counselors, friends, and God before an answer will come. And some of our questions will never be solved this side of heaven. We are not meant to know what to do. We simply have to trust the One who is the keeper of our hearts.

Don't be afraid of life! God has given it to us to be celebrated fully.

> There is a tide in the affairs of men,
> Which, taken at the flood leads on to fortune;
> Omitted, all the voyage of their life
> Is bound in shallows and in miseries.
> On such a full sea are we now afloat,
> And we must take the current when it serves
> Or lose our ventures.
>
> —WILLIAM SHAKESPEARE, *Julius Caesar*

part one

Listen!

1 Listen With Your Head

There are two types of listening—listening with your head and listening with your heart. While I realize that people often listen and make decisions with both heart and head, in many ways it's impossible to separate them. I want to discuss them separately, however, because I so strongly feel unless we learn how to separate the two, we won't be able to make some decisions at all. Our evaluations will be too muddled.

When I was younger, that was often my dilemma. I simply couldn't decide between what my heart felt and what my mind thought, so I did nothing. I know a lot of people like that now. They operate out of involuntary inertia, unable to differentiate between knowledge and feelings. When we live between those two poles, it's very hard to make sound decisions.

But the truth is, I do much better listening with my head than with my heart. I hate to confess that, because it's not always a good trait, and people are often reluctant to ask advice if they think they're going to receive head knowledge instead of a sweet, heartfelt response . . . but it's true. It's very easy for me to be cerebral or philosophical, and often I prefer to think than to feel because more tasks get done that way, and I love the sense of accomplishment.

Sometimes I ask the Lord to help me use my heart to think. Actually, it's an interesting dilemma because both categories are important. Scripture tells us in Proverbs 23:7, "As [a man] thinks in his heart, so is he." That verse positions the two seats of decision making together and states that out of both head and heart flow all the issues of life. Yet there have been times when it was a struggle to keep my head on straight and my emotions out of the process. That's happened to you, too, I'm sure.

Listen with Your Head in Financial Decisions

I remember when I first retired from Mobil Oil Corporation in 1987 and went to work for Insight for Living, my brother

Chuck's international radio ministry. At the same time, I was speaking in different locations that necessitated a lot of traveling, so I worked four days a week at Insight for Living and spent the rest of the time on the road.

I had hired a financial adviser a few years earlier—Carl Camp Jr., the president of Eclectic Associates, Inc.—so I talked with him about my change of employment and asked his counsel on what to do about trying to save money. Although my expenses often outweighed my income, I knew better than not to save something every month.

I was floored at what Carl advised, though, and I wasn't sure I could do it. He suggested I save 16 percent of my Insight salary and put it in Merrill Lynch stock on a monthly basis—*after* taxes, tithe, savings, and investments. I remember thinking, *Sixteen percent? Is he crazy? That only leaves me about 12 percent to live on.* When I told him my concern, he said, "Luci, you will never regret having this account. It will enable you to do something in the future you may know nothing about now. Tighten your belt on living expenses and see what the Lord does. Give it a try." Carl is a very strong believer in Jesus Christ, and I knew his counsel was centered in the Lord and certainly for my best interest, even though I had no idea I'd be able to follow through.

I thought about it for a week or so, praying fervently for God's direction. I knew it was sound advice coming from one who both loved the Lord and knew his stuff, financially, but could I pull it off? That was the question. (I found a lot of credence in it though because it sounded a lot like what my dad would have said. And Daddy never led me wrong in money matters.)

My heart wanted to say, *That's not possible, Carl. I can't live on that tight of a budget, and I'll never have any money to travel or have fun or eat out or do anything normal people do.* But my head was telling me to go for it, so I decided to listen with my head.

It was wise and a worthy challenge. In the end, I decided Carl was absolutely right. We set the plan in place, and at the end of that month I started buying Merrill Lynch stock.

Indeed, I did tighten my belt. And how! I made a very strict budget for myself and didn't deviate from it for five years . . . as long as I worked for Insight for Living. It was hard, but I kept biting the bullet, making myself save that money every month. As my balance began to slowly mount in the stock fund and as I read the monthly statements, I felt gratified that I'd listened to what my head was telling me to do, though I was greatly tempted to do otherwise. Here's the irony: when I bought my first home, the down payment came entirely from that Merrill Lynch fund. Those five years of strict financial discipline set the ball rolling for where I am today. Carl was right, and my head followed suit.

I think Carl listened to me with both his head and heart, because he knew I wanted to be a good steward of my money, and he counseled me toward that end. But I listened totally with my head because I knew if my heart ever let me get emotionally involved, I'd back out of the plan. It would feel too hard to accomplish.

Author and communicator Ralph Nichols once said, "The most basic of all human needs is to understand and be understood. The best way to understand people is to listen to them." Carl listened, understood, and enabled me to take wise action before I knew how to make critical financial judgments on my own. I will always appreciate him for that difficult but wise counsel. Carl has been my financial adviser for thirty-three years now, and I wouldn't think of making a big financial decision without talking with him first.

Listen with Your Head to the Scriptures

One of the greatest areas where listening with my head truly changes my life is when I read and apply the Bible. Learning the doctrines of God's Word as a young adult changed my entire way of thinking regarding a personal walk with Christ. Prior to that time, I had listened entirely with my heart regarding Scripture. If something felt good or helpful, I made decisions based on that feeling alone. But the problem was, I never seemed to grow up. I kept repeating and applying the same verses about salvation, knowing nothing about theological truth or doctrinal precepts. And I kept making the same mistakes.

When I faced issues in my life I didn't understand, I felt trapped. Since I was already a Christian and knew by heart verses regarding evangelism, I quoted those to myself—but they didn't sustain me when the chips were down and I was feeling insecure. Some of my issues were very private or too embarrassing to discuss with anyone else, so I went along, not knowing what to do. All the while, I had a wealth of information at my fingertips that could have changed the course of my life, but I didn't know how to learn it and apply it to these situations. I did everything according to how I felt because nobody encouraged me to study the Bible beyond the point of salvation.

Relationship problems, financial issues, responsibility concerns, and hardest of all . . . dealing with my own stubbornness, pride, fear, anger, disappointment, intolerance, and jealousy. I was wrapped up in my youth and uncertain about how to grow up! I had no wisdom. That was it in a nutshell. All I knew was that I had put my faith in Christ as Savior and was happy to be a Christian. But I needed

knowledge now . . . a way to make decisions that w.
sound and accurate and life changing. How was I to do that?

About this time, my parents started going to a Bible
class four nights a week, and I joined them. I was living at
home, working in Houston, and it was easy for all of us to
go together. For two years, we didn't miss a class. Attending
those Bible classes is what turned me around. I learned doctrine—the foundational truth about God's character and
how He takes care of everything about us by His grace. First
Timothy 4:16 says, "Watch your life and doctrine closely.
Persevere in them, because if you do, you will save both
yourself and your hearers" (NIV).

Believe me when I say this: had I not gone to those
Bible classes and listened with my head, I would not be
where I am today spiritually, emotionally, physically, financially, or psychologically. And I would certainly not be
speaking at Women of Faith conferences, because I would
have very little to say. Those two years of classes were the
most important years of my life. They started the maturing
process in both my head and heart.

I cannot emphasize enough the need for learning doctrine. And I can tell you for a fact that when you apply
yourself to that kind of study, listening with both heart and
head come together. They make you whole and ready for
whatever life throws your way. There is nothing else that

claim if you want to grow up, face the future,
life. It becomes one complete package that
ive life fully.

...y view, the book of the Bible that best pulls all
these thoughts together is Hebrews. About this book, my
brother Chuck says, "God is speaking to hurting Christians
on subjects about which we need to hear. He brings a
dependable, trustworthy message."

In Hebrews 6:1–3, we read what we need to do to
become mature:

> Let us stop going over the same old ground again and
> again, always teaching those first lessons about Christ.
> Let us go on instead to other things and become mature
> in our understanding, as strong Christians ought to be.
> Surely we don't need to speak further about the foolish-
> ness of trying to be saved by being good, or about the
> necessity of faith in God; you don't need further instruc-
> tion about baptism and spiritual gifts and the resurrec-
> tion of the dead and eternal judgment. The Lord
> willing, we will go on now to other things. (TLB)

Listen with Your Head in Judging the Facts

The last thing we want to become is "headstrong" when we make decisions. That would be awful. Someone who is always cold and calculating will never be able to get along in life. I've worked with people like that, and they're a pain in the neck. There is no softness or tolerance.

I can think of only one place where being headstrong might work, and that's on jury duty. I've been a juror several times and thoroughly enjoyed it, actually. It plugs into that part of me that likes to lead with my head—that part where I have to guard against intolerance. When a jury is reminded over and over to weigh all the evidence and if there is a reasonable doubt, the defendant has to be found innocent, a lot of listening to one's head comes into play.

Years ago, I served on a case in which a woman was suing a parking garage where she had fallen on the asphalt. After hearing all the facts, we went into the jury room to deliberate the case. One of the jurors was adamant about the whole thing being unfair. "Unfair" is a judgment call, and it was completely based on the juror's heartfelt perspective. The rest of us tried for a long time to get her to consider only the evidence, but it was tough. She couldn't get past how she felt about the poor individual being on trial over something that didn't seem to be her fault. We kept reminding the juror that she couldn't let her own emotions enter into the decision-making process. Finally, somebody in the room said, "Don't listen to your heart. Listen to your head . . . to the facts, the evidence. That's all you have to do. Then make a decision on that only."

That's what I mean when I say listen with your head. It's taking data and processing it through your mind in a way that brings you to a decision regardless of how you feel.

Our primary goal as mature Christians, of course, is to find a happy medium between what our heart tells us and what our head tells us without compromising obedience. Nobody totally achieves that perfect balance, but the Holy Spirit can help us with our efforts. He comes alongside us and enables us to reach a conclusion we can live with.

Without this kind of maturity in both spheres, though, we won't be able to listen to others without being critical or without being hurt. Those are the final two chapters in this section, and to achieve each takes a great deal of dependence on the Lord and getting our preferences out of the way.

2 Listen with Your Heart

I don't know how many times I've stopped for roadside lemonade this summer— three, maybe four? In my immediate neighborhood, there aren't that many children; but once you drive about two blocks, kids are all over the place. And I'd say a quarter of them have lemonade stands.

I can't resist buying a drink at a lemonade stand. There's such potentiality about that little enterprise. I always stop, because I want to encourage kids to start their own bank account, I want to honor parents for giving them their first job, and I'm thirsty. All in all, it feels like good stewardship to spend a few bucks on a cup of home-made lemonade even though it never tastes very good.

Taste, after all, is not the point. Then what is? Your heart! Your heart tells you to stop, and if you listen with your heart, you'll do it. And if the sign says "50 cents," you'll leave at least a dollar. Usually I get two glasses and leave five bucks. I'm such a sucker for lemonade stands!

Alexandra Scott came up with the idea of having a lemonade stand when she was just four years old to raise money for "her hospital." She wanted to help find a cure for a rare childhood disease that had started ravishing her body just before her first birthday, when she was diagnosed with neuroblastoma. Why would she take the time and effort to raise money by selling lemonade? "All kids want their tumors to go away," Alex said. Her parents, Jay and Liz Scott, listened to their daughter and took her up on her dream.

When advised that it might be difficult to get fifty cents per cup, Alex's tenacious response was, "I don't care. I want to do it anyway." Little did she realize what a brilliant idea she had come up with. Her parents helped her set the plan in motion, and soon signs had been painted, the stand was built, and cars were lining up on the street. Alex's sisters tipped off the local newspaper in Hartford, Connecticut (where she lived at the time), which ran a feature story on this exceptional little girl. Alex sat out at the stand taking money from one happy customer after another. And "fifty cents a glass" soon had to be abandoned because people were leaving one-, five-, ten-, and even twenty-dollar bills, not wanting change. The price was no longer a factor, because the lemonade stand became a way to donate to this very worthy cause. In a few months, Alex's stand had raised two thousand dollars. But this was only the beginning.

Over the next couple of years, lemonade stands started springing up across the country. Little by little, Alex's idea became a cottage industry, and thousands of dollars rolled in for this very worthy cause. Four years after Alex started her lemonade stand, a total of $2.5 million had been raised to help find a cure for pediatric cancer. Alex died August 1, 2004, at the age of eight, but her dream goes on; and the 2005 goal for these nationwide lemonade stands was $5 million.

There's a place on the Internet where you can hear a song written for Alex, buy a book about her incredible vision called *Alex and the Amazing Lemonade Stand*, send off for a wristband, or purchase coffee named after this brave little girl.[1] Alex's story shows that one person can make an enormous difference to thousands of others. We never know the extent of our potential outreach.

But here's how it started: her parents listened with their hearts. They heard what Alex wanted to do, worked out a way to make it happen, and helped her every way they could. Not only did all fifty states in America pick up the idea, but there are also Alex's Lemonade stands in Canada and France. "When life gives you lemons, make lemonade," Alex said. "When you have bad things, make good things." Her parents heard those words, and they put their hearts into making it a reality.

How to Listen with Your Heart

How can someone learn the fine art of listening with the heart? Let me suggest some ways.

First of all, make it a practice to listen to other people without your own agenda in mind. No matter what they say, pay attention to their words and keep your eyes on them as you drink in their sentences.

Second, don't interrupt—no matter how absurd their words, ideas, or stories may sound to you or how much you want to say something you think is vital.

Third, don't be afraid you'll forget your comment if you don't say it right now. Chances are, you won't. And if you do, your comment probably wasn't that important anyway.

And finally, don't offer an immediate solution. Many times, the key to listening with one's heart is the ability to simply hear what other people have to say without trying to help them solve anything. I've found most people want to talk; they want to process and get their feelings out, and you (at that moment) are their listening ear. They rarely want you to tell them what to do.

Remember, people tend to share only when they feel accepted. The minute somebody judges us or tries to set us straight, we clam up because we don't want to be evaluated; we want to be received, just as we are. That's all. The truth is most of us know down deep inside what to do in trying situations. It may take us awhile to get to it, but it's there . . . in our hearts. We don't live in a social climate that's conducive to listening. Most of us want to talk. Rare is the person who will listen long enough to let the person speaking figure it out for and by himself.

Proverbs 20:5 says, "Counsel in the heart of man is like deep water; but a man of understanding will draw it out" (KJV). God has put the counsel we need to hear and know within our own hearts. When He made us, He enabled us to store that wise counsel in a very deep, private place He created. It's like a deep river, running through our hearts in a place that's completely quiet and unique to each individual. When we get in touch with that, we find His counsel with a still heart and a waiting, open soul . . . without passion, desire, judgment, or opinions. It's pure and clean and from God. But how do we get in touch with that?

I believe that's where the listening heart comes into play. The "man of understanding" is the person who listens. When a person listens, God-given counsel is drawn out of the heart of the one speaking. A person with a listening heart may ask a few pertinent questions, but for the most part he just waits and listens. It's being absorbed in another person's life, his strivings and sorrows. The "man of understanding" has wisdom enough to know not to talk but to listen. He doesn't argue; he listens. He doesn't judge; he listens. He doesn't run ahead; he simply listens.

It's a funny thing about wisdom—wisdom can't be taught. When you try to communicate wisdom, you'll sound foolish; so the secret to being wise is listening. One can teach knowledge because knowledge can be communicated, but not wisdom. The Bible says we can get wisdom, we can live in wisdom, we can be fortified by wisdom, and we can do wonders through wisdom; but no one can communicate or teach wisdom. Wisdom comes from living life, not from trying to explain life.

Therefore, if we want to be wise, we will listen with our heart—to others, to sounds, to words, to life itself. And in so doing, our heart will grow bigger, enabling us to be of more help to others in their needs.

Life! Celebrate It

The Lasting Results of Listening

When I was about ten, I decided to run away from home. I'd been planning it in my little brain for about a week and had taken a small suitcase off the closet shelf, opened it on my bed, and began packing—a few clothes, a few books, a few toys, and my favorite scrapbook from Momo, my grandmother. As I was making progress, my dad walked by the door, saw what I was doing, and came in. He sat on the end of the bed.

"What's up?" he asked.

"I'm leaving, Daddy. I don't want to live here anymore."

"OK," he said, very calmly looking at my suitcase. "But what happened to make you want to do this?" He was genuinely concerned . . . ever so sweet and eager to know what had upset me.

"I never get to do anything my way. I don't like the food here. I'm sick of always having to mind. There are too many rules. It's a bunch of stuff . . . so I'm running away!" My voice was cracking.

"Where will you eat, honey?" he asked. "Who will love you when you're sick? What will you do when you run out of money?"

I reminded him I had my two-dollar allowance.

"Two dollars won't go very far," he said. "But if you're determined to go, I'll help you pack. In fact, I'll go with you."

Well. That was worse! *Daddy wants me to go,* I thought, *or he wouldn't offer to help.* It was a very confusing moment. I was stuck in a dilemma and needed something to change, but I didn't know what. I just wanted relief from my childish predicament and thought running away would do it.

After talking with my dad for a while, though, and having him pay such thoughtful attention to my heart with his heart, I felt better and finally settled down and unpacked.

My father had no idea what wisdom he showed at that moment, but it affected me for life. His love entrusted me with a sense of security. Because he wanted to go with me wherever I went, he modeled what God was like—that He would never leave me. To this day, I can travel unafraid all over the world because my daddy instilled in me assurance by his love and by hearing me out. It was an unforgettable moment.

When we listen with our hearts, it's amazing how the action taken as a result can alter people's lives forever. As we hear the needs and longings of others, we are moved to do something to help them. This is the philosophy behind Habitat for Humanity International. In this creative partnership, those of us who want to help find a means to do so.

Habitat for Humanity is a nonprofit, Christian housing ministry that works to eliminate poverty housing around the world and to offer those who need adequate housing an opportunity to have it through homeowner partners. Homeowners are selected by local affiliates based upon their need for housing, their ability to repay a nonprofit mortgage, and their willingness to partner with Habitat. This organization started in 1976 by Linda and Millard Fuller. It was dedicated to eliminating substandard housing and homelessness worldwide. Fuller's book *Love in the Mortar Joints* proved that his idea was workable, and Habitat for Humanity has provided homes for more than one million people to date.[2]

In May 2005, Women of Faith had a chance to join with one of the branches of Habitat, called Women Build, to help build a house in Dallas that had been bought by a young family in need. When we arrived at the workplace, the number of people already there and hard at work blew me away. Three Habitat homes were being built at the same time, and the one we worked on had been constructed entirely by women. I thought it was remarkable. This type of construction is being done all over the world.

Much like Alex's Lemonade, Habitat for Humanity has its own Web page. It offers opportunities to be part of a "volunteer vacation" in a Global Village, the Habitat for Humanity University, where one can explore new courses online; and campus chapters and youth programs, where young people can be involved in building around the world. It even tells you how you can hook up with a Habitat RV team to build houses and friendships when you're on the road.[3]

I keep a picture in my journal of a family whose home I helped build with my donations. When I see that picture, I'm reminded that anything is possible when we listen with our hearts. There's no end to ideas and possibilities when people listen to each other and really want to help. Anything is possible with God—when we choose to listen to Him.

3 Listen without Being Critical

My grandfather had a charming little bay cottage in Texas, and our family often visited there on summer vacations. I have to say it was rare when we weren't in church on Sundays during our visits, because Mother sang in the choir, Daddy was an usher, we kids were involved in youth activities, and Granddaddy taught a men's Bible class. As far back as I can remember, church was an active part of our weekends, both at home and on vacation.

Nevertheless, for some reason we had gone fishing one particular Sunday. A great time was had by all out in that little boat, bobbing around and waiting for the fish to bite. It was the most natural thing in the world for me to be on such an excursion, because as kids, we grew up with a pole in one hand and bait bucket in the other.

The problem with this trip came the following weekend when we went back to Sunday school. In front of the class, my teacher asked why I wasn't there the week before. When I innocently reported I'd been fishing with my family at the bay, the teacher asked, "Do you think God can bless you when you miss Sunday school just to go fishing?" I had no idea what to do with that question, and I can't remember how I answered it (if I did), but I'll never forget how her question made me feel. I was embarrassed and felt ashamed. I didn't understand the criticism, but I definitely internalized it.

Leave the Judging to God

Criticism is one of the hardest things to take and one of the easiest things to give. Unless we listen with our hearts we can find a hundred reasons to criticize other people—how they dress; what they drive; where they shop, travel, or go to church; their values, political beliefs, sexual or philosophical lifestyle; their thoughts on any given issue; their home, family life, husband, wife, children . . . right down to how they part their hair.

Jesus has a lot to say about being critical or judgmental.

Listen to His words from the first few verses in Matthew 7:

> Don't pick on people, jump on their failures, criticize
> their faults—unless, of course, you want the same
> treatment. That critical spirit has a way of boomerang-
> ing. It's easy to see a smudge on your neighbor's face
> and be oblivious to the ugly sneer on your own. Do
> you have the nerve to say, 'Let me wash your face for
> you,' when your own face is distorted by contempt?
> It's this whole traveling road-show mentality all over
> again, playing a holier-than-thou part instead of just
> living your part. Wipe that ugly sneer off your own
> face, and you might be fit to offer a washcloth to your
> neighbor. (vv. 1–5 MSG)

Jesus is adamant about anyone passing judgment on
another human being. He says, "Don't be nitpickers; use
your head—and heart!—to discern what is right, to test
what is authentically right" (John 7:24 MSG).

In these passages, Jesus is telling us not to be "picky,
picky, picky." But we all are to some degree. Nitpickers find
fault and criticism with everything they encounter, and
they're a curse in the household of faith. They're maddening to the human race and *especially* to the body of Christ.
Jesus is the only one qualified to judge, because He's the

only One who sees our hearts and listens with His. Our judgment of another is no better than the information we have (or think we have), but Jesus knows us better than we know ourselves. He has the total picture.

The most tragic example in my personal experience of someone being criticized instead of listened to happened to a dear friend of mine many, many years ago. I was taking voice lessons from this man (let's call him Bob), and we had become friends through our fifteen years of singing together in the Opera Chorus. He had a beautiful baritone voice and was a delight to know; he was fun, charming, sensitive, and a complete gentleman. Bob was a vocal coach by profession, but the chorus brought us together on rehearsal nights when we'd often go out afterward to sit and talk for hours over coffee. I was much younger then and could stay up half the night chatting away and go to work the next morning, unaffected by lack of sleep. Ah! Those were the days.

Bob was in his thirties, unmarried, lived alone, and loved to read. Often, we talked about books and what each of us was learning at the time. On occasion, we'd be reading the same thing, so the discussions often went from amicable to hot in no time. Great fun! Bob had a quick, sharp, witty mind and always challenged me in my beliefs and thoughts. I loved this guy. One night, he confided in me that he was gay and was battling with patterns and behavior in his life that were contrary to his Christian convictions. He said he felt unable to overcome this pull on his heart but didn't want homosexuality to define his lifestyle. I understood and empathized.

Bob attended a local church in his neighborhood where he was actively involved in the music program and often told me about his friends in that church with whom he'd have dinner and visit in "surface table conversation," as he called it. "It's not like *our* visits, Luci," he'd say. "You and I have a more balanced, deeper friendship, but these folks are sort of my 'church support group,' I guess. I feel like I can talk to them, and I'm thinking of telling them I'm gay. What do you think?"

I asked why he wanted to do that, and he responded, "Well, lately I've really been struggling with my feelings about this certain guy, and I'd like my friends to pray for me. They don't know me very well, but they seem tolerant, and I think I'm OK with telling them."

I cautioned Bob to be careful with whom he shared this information. "You'd better know what you're doing," I said. "Some Christians feel very called to correct, and they could have a heyday with this. Just be sure before you give them enough fuel to start a fire."

Apparently, at one of these "surface table conversations,"

Bob was unusually troubled over his feelings of guilt, so he opened his heart to his church buddies. He told them about his sexual persuasion, feelings, and fears. He confessed his struggle about being both gay and a Christian. But instead of being supportive, his friends condemned him. They said they questioned his commitment to Christ if he had those kinds of feelings. They quoted a bunch of scriptures and responded to Bob's honesty by criticizing and judging him. When Bob shared all this with me at our next late-night visit, I was sick at heart. Appalled. Mad. I wanted somehow to get them banned from the church roll. But, that was minor compared to what happened next.

As if their condemnation weren't enough, they told the senior pastor of their church. Bob was publicly reprimanded so he could set about "cleaning up his life and thoughts." A few days later, on a Tuesday evening, Bob phoned to tell me about the pastor's now being involved. I could hardly believe it. This was a travesty (a "road-show mentality," as Eugene Peterson puts it in *The Message*), and it was happening in the church.

Added to my friend's deep fears regarding his sexual orientation, there was now the added debilitating concern of public exposure. Bob told me he felt like he was drowning. He cried on the phone . . . and so did I. I prayed for him as we talked, and just before he hung up, he said he would always regret telling those "so-called Christians" his deepest secret. I didn't blame him. I was furious and had to ask God to forgive me for what I wanted to do to that crowd of Pharisees.

I remember saying to Bob that I felt certain there would be no public reprimand. That would be barbaric, and we lived in the twentieth century. It just wouldn't happen . . . so he should try to keep the faith and trust the Lord. I said everything I could think of to encourage him to hang on. "Don't give up; you'll win out over this. You're much bigger than that mob of thieves who have stolen your reputation." But apparently everything I said fell on deaf ears.

The following Friday night about eight o'clock, there was a knock at my front door. When I opened it, there stood a man whom I didn't know well but recognized as someone I had met through Bob. He, too, was a musician in the same church my friend attended. I felt a chill run up my spine when I saw him. His face was full of anguish and nervousness, and he said in a flat, solemn voice as he walked through the door, "Luci, Bob is dead."

I couldn't move. I'm sure the color left my face as I stared at the man and said nothing. Finally I sat down, shocked and grieved. Everything was totally silent. It seemed even the clock stopped. Never taking his eyes off me, the man continued after a few moments: "Earlier this evening, Bob lay down on his bed, put a gun in his mouth, and blew his head off."

Although this happened forty-five years ago, I can feel everything I felt that unspeakable night as though it happened yesterday. I thought I would collapse. A million bells started clanging in my head as I heard my mouth saying, " . . . blew his head off . . . blew his head off." I simply couldn't believe it; there was no place in my heart to slot this information and make it fit. "I just talked with him this week," I muttered after a few minutes. Then I remembered Bob's very real fears and the terror in his voice the previous Tuesday night. When the whole truth of what I'd been told finally hit me, I sank into the chair with sorrow and cried for hours and hours and hours. Such a senseless loss.

A few days later, I attended Bob's funeral. It was a cold, unfeeling, plastic ceremony of paying final respects. Nothing about it had any warmth or heart. I, too, was only there as a matter of protocol to somehow pay a final homage to my dear friend. I knew nobody in attendance. All I could do was grieve silently in my own little space. I kept thinking of Bob's wonderful spirit that was now on the other side of this life.

One thing that happened, though, I'll never forget. Seated a few feet away from me was Bob's mother, a dear old woman dressed in black and broken in spirit. As the eulogy was read and the organ was played, she occasionally whispered to no one in particular, "Why?" It was a tormented, quiet cry of a heart that was left to wonder about the untimely and inexplicable death of her son. But to me it was an echo across the ages of time for all those who have been maligned, misunderstood, judged, and condemned because they dared to be transparent with someone who criticized instead of listened. Why?

The issue in this story is not homosexuality. It's not any act of sin or behavior that takes away our peace with God. It's the lack of understanding and kindness on the part of those of us who know better when we respond with judgment about something that is only God's to judge. Sometimes insensitivity of the Christian community is harder for me to accept than the unbeliever who refuses to put his faith in the Savior.

When people are hurting and need our support, our love, and our listening ear, let's be there for them. When admonition is required, let's approach that by showing the same tolerance for others that we want shown to us, and when judgment is the best answer . . . let's leave that to God.

Look Within Your Own Heart

I confess to you, there are times I would rather stay holed up in my house than deal with other people and their judgmental natures beyond these doors. Then I remind myself that I, too, can fall into this category easier than I care to admit. Part of the human condition is to be prejudiced and criticize those who are not like us. We're all looking for a place to be totally accepted just as we are, without criticism from others. Does it exist? No, I don't think so.

We all want to be in a church body or group of friends or with a support team that will stand with us when we're facing an earth-shattering issue in our own lives. Especially if it's a private thing—struggling with homosexuality, going through a divorce, having an abortion, being involved in an affair, running from the law—any of those things qualify. And more.

We all want somebody in our lives who won't pass judgment. I think we pass judgment on ourselves, which is hard enough for us to deal with without having the neighborhood or church body join in.

Nobody has answers to these dilemmas. There are always more questions than answers. And nobody has the best advice to give. We're all students of life with its confusing struggles. Let's try to be patient with each other, giving the benefit of the doubt and waiting for the Lord to work in the lives of those we love, while we give our prayerful support.

Remember these words written by George Washington Carver, a Negro slave in the 1800s: "How far you go in life depends on your being tender with the young, compassionate with the aged, sympathetic with the striving, and tolerant of the weak and the strong. Because someday in life you will have been all of these."

4 Listen When You're Hurt

Before I worked for Women of Faith, I spent fifteen years traveling and speaking by myself. I knew most of the other speakers who are now on the Women of Faith core team, but each of us traveled independently of the other. During those days, I often met other women with whom I spoke just for a weekend or a special event. Patsy Clairmont occasionally gave book reviews where I delivered a message, and I was always thrilled when she was part of the program because nobody reviewed a book as beautifully or entertainingly as she. But our paths rarely crossed otherwise. Marilyn Meberg and I were dear friends, but we didn't speak at the same meetings.

However, there was a woman with whom I frequently shared the podium, and we became friends through several years of working together. On occasion, we visited one another in our respective homes and knew each other's families. In other words, we had a sweet relationship apart from our public ministry together. There were many times we had long conversations and wonderful laughter, and I treasured my friend dearly. I still do, in fact, although our paths haven't crossed in a long time.

After a number of years of sharing the platform in a speaking ministry, my friend confronted me about something she didn't like in my speaking style. I saw her as a gifted communicator with wonderful depth and value to her words, and I admired her greatly. I often told her how encouraged I was when she spoke, and I genuinely praised her ability with words. As you can imagine, I was greatly surprised by her confrontation.

When she shared her thoughts about my messages, I was hurt deeply. She was speaking as my friend (which qualified her to voice her opinion, of course) and had enough experience herself to make a bona fide evaluation. Nonetheless, her words were painful to hear.

First of all, I knew there must be truth to her comments, since someone I loved and respected as a public speaker herself spoke them. Second, I felt embarrassed when she told me because I viewed myself as a "seasoned" speaker and wondered why someone hadn't brought this to my attention earlier. And finally . . . I felt sort of empty that I hadn't recognized this problem in myself. After all, I was a mature believer—one who had walked with the Lord for many, many years. I had lots of communication experience under my belt from college, from my work with Mobil Oil, from years of public speaking. Was it a blind spot? Was I just dense?

That episode in my life was very difficult because I internalized the words of my friend, and it distanced me from her until I could work through the pain. I held hard feelings for many months but finally came to the realization that "wounds from a friend are better than kisses from an enemy," as Proverbs 27:6 (TLB) says.

I finally decided to do my own personal Bible study on being hurt, offended, or resentful. God's Spirit showed me I was wrong to take offense. Psalm 119:165 reads, "Great peace have they which love thy law: and nothing shall offend them" (KJV). Oh brother! *Nothing* shall offend us? While that's the ideal for every believer in Christ, it's something we all have to work toward. When we're offended, it's difficult to come back to the place we started . . . a neutral place is hard to find in situations like that.

There's another proverb that reads, "It's harder to win

back the friendship of an offended brother than to capture a fortified city. His anger shuts you out like iron bars" (18:19 TLB). That's the way I felt about my friend who had hurt me. I simply backed off and wanted to stay there. Even though she knew I was crushed over her words, I didn't contact her. Even though she made every effort to apologize and explain herself further, I didn't listen. Even though she meant her criticism to be helpful, I didn't take it that way. It wasn't that I necessarily wanted to punish her; it was that I was too ashamed and embarrassed to approach her and try to discuss things. No matter how deliberate and loving her attempts, we remained estranged for a long time. It was as if something in me clicked off, and I stayed aloof.

I've never forgotten that experience, and although we have now regained much of the ground we lost, I find I'm more cautious around her. I'm sure I don't need to be distant as far as she's concerned, but something in me feels distance. I wish it were not so, but it is. Maybe my guard is up because I'm not hurt very often; and when I am, it sinks very deeply into my soul, taking me a long time to work it out.

In spite of that, the experience sobered me and made me want to heed her input. That was my friend's gift to me, and in many ways, it changed my entire approach to a public speaking ministry.

Helpful Actions When You've Been Hurt

"We cannot afford to forget any experience, not even the most painful," Dag Hammarskjöld once said. He was a brilliant man—an outstanding leader who, as the former secretary general of the United Nations, worked closely with men and women from all over the world.

When we think about the relationships in our lives—friends and acquaintances, family members, co-workers, or fellow students—is there anybody who has hurt you by what they've said? Their words might have been an offhanded comment or a momentary attack. Their words might have been just an aside, but they sting deeply and leave us reeling. I don't think it's possible to be in the human condition and escape the sting of words. Times come in our lives when something heard is too harsh, too devastating, too pointed, or too critical. It's impossible not to be hurt.

This chapter is about *listening* when you feel hurt. It's about taking heed to what you're hearing, although it may be painful to listen to. I want to suggest a few principles that often help me when I'd rather react or attack instead of listening to the one who makes me feel chided. These are only suggestions; when I have applied them, they've worked for me. Although the pain may not go away immediately (or maybe ever), the effort to apply helpful actions sees us through and keeps us from giving up on that other individual. Consider these six ideas that might also work for you:

First, *let the person finish talking before you say anything.* Sometimes all the other person wants is to make her point known. She wants to get it off her chest. Maybe she's been carrying this feeling around for a long time, eager to tell you what's driving her crazy but hasn't had the courage to spit it out; so let her do that.

Second, *state back to the person what you think she said.* We can easily misunderstand what's been communicated, so try to repeat to the other person what you heard. If that is *not* what she meant, ask her to tell you again so you both agree the same message has been delivered and understood.

Third, *own what you believe to be true about her words.* This is one of the hardest things in the world to do. Take it from one who knows. It is very, very difficult to see our own faults; therefore, it's almost impossible to own our own troublesome behavior in relationships. If we can't see it, we can't own it. Tell your confronter that you will pray about it, and then ask God to show you so you can set it right for your *own* sake as well as hers. After all, it's not your desire to go through life hurting people. As Scripture says, if you love God's law, you don't want to be offended (Psalm 119:165) . . . and you certainly don't want to offend.

Fourth, *thank her for being honest with you.* Remember, it's the truth that sets us free, and if we can all get to the truth in relationships, we can overcome a lot of potential problems. We're looking for ways to make peace and keep it.

Fifth, *try not to personalize what is not your problem.* This is something I honestly weigh carefully when somebody talks to me about what troubles them and hurts me. For example, let's say someone is snippy, short-tempered, or petty with you. If this is their pattern with other friends or family members, more than likely it is not your problem. It's a pattern that's characteristic of their behavioral history. Unfortunately, they direct it to others, and you fall under that cloud. It might hurt you, but it need not. Just thank the person for telling you and go on your way. Don't waste time pointing out you've seen her do this to others. Why start a little feud? Just get out of her way. This is not the place to list her faults that drive you nuts too. Get beyond it.

Finally, *pray with the person to whom you have been listening.* I don't always do this, but when I do I'm glad—especially if it is a very close loved one. I want to get closure, and how better to do that than to invite the Lord to help you?

A Love That Is Not Easily Offended

When I was in the process of building my house, my friend Ney Bailey, who lives in my neighborhood, was kind enough to walk around many times with the builder and give my instructions to him since I had to be out of town so much with Women of Faith. She graciously represented me in almost every major decision of this whole project, and she did a superb job. (If the truth were known, Ney could be a builder in her own right. She knows the trade, the people involved, and the problems with new construction; and she enjoys every aspect of the project itself.) I relied heavily on her expertise during those many months when my house was being built.

I recall one occasion when Ney telephoned me while I was in another state, asking me to make an immediate decision regarding the edging that was being put around two of my front windows. She felt it was the wrong color and not what I had chosen months earlier at the design center. The call came at a time I was in a rental car, in heavy traffic, and in no mood to make such an important decision over the phone. I needed time to think about what was going on and try to reconstruct those windows in my mind's eye before I advised Ney what to do.

I'm sure she could hear frustration in my voice. I responded with kind of an irritated tone, which resulted in hard feelings between us for a few days. I didn't take time to listen to everything that was being said and I got put out with her for cornering me in that position. Mind you, it's virtually impossible to be irritated at or hurt by Ney for very long, because she exhibits the fruit of the Spirit almost constantly; so I was sure the problem was totally mine. I was short tempered and hurried and needed to concentrate on managing traffic instead of deciding on the color of window trim. It was just poor timing all around.

Parenthetically, these are the kinds of inconsequential, nagging misunderstandings that tick us off and keep us apart from the people we love most because we feel hurt by them. These are everyday problems that cause angst, rancor, enmity . . . anything that makes us feel hurt inside.

I made a decision hurriedly over the phone (in spite of not wanting to) and told Ney to be sure of what I had initially chosen and then advise them to use that color, even if it had to be changed to make it right. She followed up and took care of the whole thing. As it turned out, the color was indeed wrong, and had it not been for Ney, my window trim would have been black instead of the beige I ordered.

I was living in Ney's guest room at the time, waiting for my house to be completed, so when I got back to Texas she asked if we could talk. I was reluctant, because I hate confrontation and didn't want to feel my feelings about what had happened. But I agreed, and one evening we discussed the whole misunderstanding. She was as sweet as could be and, as usual, totally gracious. She didn't get mad or raise her voice or talk over me or down to me. She was just as she always is—full of the Spirit of God . . . kind, long-suffering, and exceedingly patient. Ney applied almost all those suggestions I listed earlier in this chapter.

I was impressed and moved by her spirit, and after we worked out our differences and reached an understanding, we never had another problem about the house. We've looked back on that time with laughter and pathos, remembering what we learned about each other . . . and about the trials of building a house. Our friendship goes on!

I asked Ney that night why she was so good at making peace when feelings were hurt in relationships. She said, "Well, Luci, I've learned that if you take care of things between yourself and someone else 'a brick at a time,' you'll never build a wall." I should say so.

Ney's response to me characterizes the gentle, logical, calm approach to talking, listening, and hearing even if we're hurt. It's sweet and full of love. Not the namby-pamby kind of love that serves as a front for just wanting to get through something painful, but the real, solid-rock love that Christ gives us when we want to find peace in loving His law so that nothing will offend us.

part two

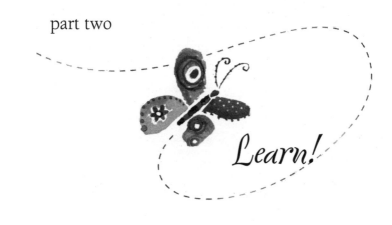

Learn!

5 Learn What to Save

The speakers at Women of Faith are often asked, "How do you do all you do? How can you travel weekend after weekend without a break?" If you were to look deeply into each one of our lives, you'd see that speaking at Women of Faith conferences is only one of the things we do, albeit the most public part of our schedule. In addition to preparing and delivering speeches, we also do interviews, appear on television, write books, visit bookstores for book signings, go to photo and video shoots, write letters, do voiceovers, and attend Women of Faith association meetings and team meetings. Not to mention travel. In some cases—depending on the speaker—we also prepare for and speak at the preconference, record music CDs, write and present dramatic sketches, and speak at fund-raisers or other extracurricular functions. (I have the feeling I've left out something!)

All in all, being a part of the Women of Faith speaking team is one of the most time-consuming, challenging journeys of my life. And it is one of the most delightfully satisfying. Before I got here, I had retired twice! "And this is your eleventh year at this pace?" you ask. Yes. Of course, the duties have become more complex annually, but as far back as I can remember, I've been up to my ears in work obligations.

Oh, here's what I forgot: in addition to all our professional and ministry responsibilities, each of us also has a personal life—a life with families and friends and our own hobbies and activities. We go to church and read books and see movies and have dinner parties and celebrate birthdays and give showers and keep house and go on vacation. We rear children, play with our grandchildren, and go to PTA meetings and board meetings. We pay bills, go shopping, and get haircuts, manicures, pedicures, and massages (or wish we could!). We write e-mails, respond to requests, make decisions, pray, read our Bibles, face difficulties and losses, show up for the unexpected, bathe, eat, sleep, and do laundry.

If the truth were known, our lives are much like yours—

filled to the brim with the good, the bad, and the time consuming. Every woman I know has a ton of stuff to do, and before she can turn around, she's asked to do something more, something else, something different. There's no end to the demands upon women. It may be a different scenario for a Women of Faith speaker, but wherever you are in life, you're faced with the same requirement for the body, mind, and spirit.

Save the Right Things

So how do we manage? Well, let's see. I can't answer for anyone else (although I could give you a pretty accurate, educated guess), but I can answer for me: I've learned what to save. I'm not a master at the fine art of saving, but I'm getting better as I get older. After a lot of years of trial and error, I'm learning what to keep and what to throw out.

I start with evaluation. I ask myself a series of questions: What do I want most? How badly do I want it? Is it worth the price (time, energy, or money)? Do I have a place for it—in my house or my heart? Will I want it a year from now? I go through a whole rigmarole of questions. Actually, it's a pretty academic exercise that I can do rapidly, since I've done it for so long. And most importantly, I try to keep my emotions out of the decision.

Once this exercise is underway, I begin to picture where I'm going to keep what I want. Here's where the fun starts. There are times when I want something just for the fun of having it, even though I'll have to build a room on to find a place for it.

The day after I moved into my new house in 2004, I received 527 pounds of stickers and photo albums (a total of sixteen boxes) delivered to my front door. They were all from Mrs. Grossman's Paper Company. Andrea Grossman is a gifted artist and personal friend of mine, and her stickers, papers, and albums are the best in the world. Right after my house was completed, I had a cabinet built in my little studio just for stickers, the majority of which are Andrea's. The cabinet has eight easy-opening drawers and two shelves. Beautiful! Needless to say, I was beside myself when these boxes arrived! *What a housewarming gift*, I thought. *And what timing; I just moved in yesterday and look at this. That Andrea! It's fabulous.*

There was a gang of people helping me arrange furniture and put things away, so we stopped in our tracks and immediately began to tear into these sixteen new boxes. I looked at everything between squeals and shouts and labeled each box with its contents and where they would finally go. In my mental evaluation file, I knew full well I didn't *really* have room for all this stuff, but I wanted it, would want it a year from now, and would somehow find a place for it. I could hardly wait to hold it all in my hands and wallow in it. I felt rich and loved the extravagance of my bountiful stickers.

Among my helpers that day was my dear friend Kathy Short (on staff with Women of Faith) and her adorable ten-year-old daughter, McKenzie. McKenzie is a tender-hearted, soulful, verbal child and a sweet friend of mine. She and I were shrieking with laughter, singing, and clapping as we wildly discussed all the things we'd do with these stickers once we had everything displayed before us. Of course, I promised her piles and piles of them.

After this went on about forty-five minutes, we started to realize something was fishy. We began to notice that not only was this too much—it was too much of the same thing! Dozens of photo albums the same color and size; hundreds of extra pages for each album; boxes and boxes of nothing but Christmas stickers . . . on and on. "Could all this have come to you by mistake?" someone asked. I stopped labeling (and squealing) and asked Jenny Clay, another friend and Women of Faith staff member, who was categorizing everything into a final list, to call Mrs. Grossman's Paper Company and see if they had sent an order of this magnitude recently and if it might have accidentally gotten to me. She did so and learned that's exactly what happened. The shipment was supposed to have gone to a sticker store in Oregon, not to my house. It was to be part of their Christmas inventory. Oh, no!

A pall fell over my whole house. It got very quiet. In my mind, I had categorized, alphabetized, and stored every piece of paper and every sticker. In little McKenzie's mind, she had taken home her treasures and played with them for days and weeks ahead. Never mind that I really needed none of it. We all stared at each other speechlessly.

After a bit, McKenzie said quietly but profoundly, "I feel sad." I knew exactly what she meant, and I felt it too. It's a feeling I know well. In the sad truth of the moment, we had to admit all that we thought was ours had just slipped through our fingers.

This feeling is part of every human heart. Wanting something wonderful to last starts when we're children. McKenzie is ten, and I'm in my seventies, yet we both wanted this treasure to be ours. No matter our age, we always want the good to last. And we always want more. (I once asked a very rich man how much is enough, and he answered, "Enough is always a little bit more than you have.")

As we began to figure out how we were going to get these boxes sealed up again and to their rightful owner, McKenzie asked us why she felt sad. She knew her heart was aching over a sense of loss, but she had no place to slot it. I said to her, "McKenzie, this is a feeling you'll have often, because life rarely lives up to our expectations. But that's OK, as long as we remember it won't. I want you to remember something else, though. It's that other feeling—the one of celebration . . . when we were yelling and singing. Hang on to that. Even for a few split seconds, we had fun and joy—and that's just as much a part of life as the disappointment. Don't miss it . . . and always look for it."

That scenario showed me again how hard it is to limit one's self to enough. When is enough, enough? Sometimes our eyes are bigger than our capacity to store or to enjoy the stuff we want. With all the stickers I already had in my cabinet, I wanted 527 pounds more. The insatiable human heart! It's hard to learn contentment. Ironically, the most genuinely contented people I know have very little. They've learned what to save and what to give away, and their hearts are typically very generous.

Save the Old and the New

Logistically speaking, when we talk about learning what to save, I think we need a set of organizing principles to work from. For me, Martha Stewart takes the prize. Regardless of what you think of her personally, you have to agree that her organizational ideas are revolutionary. Some of them may be a little over the top, but for a person as busy as she, I admire her ability to keep her sanity. I've ordered from her catalogs many times and never regretted a single purchase. So if you want advice on how to organize your household, she's my first choice.

One trick I've noticed: she puts the old with the new, the tattered with the polished, the toys with the china . . . and makes it all look wonderful and doable. What she can do with boxes, binders, books, and bulletin boards is amazing. She shows me time and time again that I can mix and match everything. On top of an armoire, I've displayed a 1939 painting by my aunt alongside a modern piece of sculpture . . . and it works. I'd love to call Martha when I get ready to do my landscaping! Never shy away from eccentric designers. They're among the best.

Save the Odds and Ends

What about all those little notes and scraps of paper that are precious to you and nobody else—old pictures, report cards, and love letters that you can't seem to part with? Should you save them? Oh, yes! My life is made up of little scraps. I'm kind of like Virginia Woolf, who said, "I might in the course of time learn what it is that one can make of this loose, drifting material of life; finding another use for it." So I save all of it.

Most of my threads and pieces of life's driftwood are in journals. There are dozens of them I've written and kept for years. Attached to these pages are those scraps with which I could never seem to part—odds and ends I often fling in there without thinking twice. And you'd be amazed how many times I've relied on those entries and flotsam to give somebody directions or answer a question for a friend who couldn't remember a date or facts. I like to come back to them in months or years to figure out if anything has changed. We need to save things that define our personal world because it validates who we are. It's our drifting material of life. In my collection are not only my journals but those of my mother and grandmother. I have library shelves full of our journals.

When Marilyn's daughter, Beth, was twelve years old (she's in her thirties now), she gave me a little paper mask she had made in school. It was constructed with big eyes, curly hair, a darling nose, and big red cheeks. I've had it for twenty-four years, and nothing could make me part with it. It hangs on my studio wall, and I see it every day. It's one of my tiny treasures.

I remember sitting at the kitchen table when I was a little girl, talking with my mother while she peeled potatoes for dinner. I don't want to ever forget those moments. They're hidden in my savings-account mental file and will be forever. This is why I save material stuff. It gives shape to the narrative of my life. I trust my instincts on what's important and put it away for keeps. Amazingly, these scraps and bits are the fodder for my writing, my stories and messages . . . and what you hang on to will be the same for you. Wasn't it Flannery O'Connor who said something like, "If we survive childhood, we'll have something to write about the rest of our lives"?

Save Money

Finally, one of the most important lessons I've learned about saving has to do with saving money. The first time I was made aware of money was when I got a two-dollar allowance per week. My father gave each of his three kids that two-dollar allowance for chores we did around the house. I saved nothing. Ever. In fact, I had to borrow money from my brothers when I wanted to buy anything, because I spent mine the minute it got in my hand.

After I borrowed enough from the boys to get two balsa wood models from the hobby store, my dad thought it was time to give me a lesson on the proper use of money. It's one of the finest pieces of information he ever gave me, and I still apply those principles today. He held up one hand with his fingers spread wide apart, and with the other hand he pointed to each finger. "Honey," he said, "with every dollar you make, if you save some, spend some, tithe some, invest some, and give some away . . . you'll always have money and you'll always enjoy money. It won't own you; you'll own it."

I can't tell you the times I've applied that advice and kept my head above water financially because of it. And it works no matter what you make. Learning how to save money has nothing to do with the amount of your paycheck. It has to do with the ability to live within your means and delegate where different parts of that check go.

Having a savings account is one of those parts. It sounds too simplistic, but it works. And the more you put in it, the better you learn how it's done successfully. If you save long enough, it gets to be second nature; it's a wonderful habit and the key by which you can open doors to many things you want to do—travel, go to school, buy a home, and help others. On and on and on.

Uh-oh. Now I'm talking about spending. I didn't mean to get off on that. See how easy it is to spend what we mean to save? Too easy. But we'll also have money to spend when we apply Daddy's method. I promise.

6 Learn What to Spend

$\mathcal{S}$ ara Teasdale once wrote:

> Spend all you have for loveliness,
>   Buy it and never count the cost;
> For one white singing hour of peace
>   Count many a year of strife well lost.[1]

What a beautiful thought! I love the poem from which this is taken, called "Barter." To *barter* is to trade commodities. If you spend everything for loveliness, according to this poem, you'll trade a year of turmoil for an hour of peace. I'd love to be able to do that sometimes, especially on days when I can't take on one more responsibility. But life doesn't work that way, even though I like to toy with the philosophy. Dreaming about it transports me to another plane and makes me calm for a while. That's what poetry often does for us . . . it takes us out of the present.

Life does give us resources that we can use to barter, however. They come in three forms—time, energy, and money. Each is the medium of exchange for something we want in its place. It's kind of funny, really:. When we're young, we have time and energy but little money. When we're middle aged, we have money and energy, but little time. And when we're old, we have time and money, but little energy. At least, that's what it feels like. Would that there was a way to have all three at once. Is there? Maybe so . . . at least to some degree.

Be a Steward of Your Time

Take *time*, for example. It's my highest priority right now. I never have enough of it. When I look back through thirty years of journaling, on almost every page I've written something about not having enough time. And the truth is, I'll never have enough time because it's all up to God, and He views time differently than I do.

My time has to do with *duration*, a measurable period when something occurs. I don't have enough "duration" during the day. I lack the continuum for everything I want or need to do to actually get it done. It's that simple. But God's timing is in terms of *division*; He operates moment by moment or through seasons or a lifetime or a dispensation. His time is not measurable, because He's eternal and earthly time is temporal.

The reason this is important is because when I look at my life from a human viewpoint, I run out of time. But when I look at it from a spiritual viewpoint, I see that God is in charge of everything; I'm not! Therefore, He's in charge of my time. "My times are in Your hand," the psalmist says (31:15). You could read that, "My *divisions* are in Your hand." Therefore, I will accomplish whatever comes my way even though it may not be written into the schedule of my daily planner. Eugene Petersen translates that verse, "Hour by hour I place my days in your hand" (MSG).

Realistically speaking, then, I do have enough time. I have all the time God wants me to have and can spend it any way I like. But here's where I get hung up—it's up to me to find the best way to spend my time, and sometimes I don't choose the best. My problem is I forget this and am inclined to blame somebody else for my lack of time. They've given me too many duties, interrupted me, demanded too much, or required a deadline I can't meet—

or so I think. In reality, though, lack of time is my own fault. I just need to learn how to spend it better.

Be a Steward of Your Energy

What about energy? The dictionary defines *energy* as the vigorous exertion of power. It has to do with effort, strength, potency, and might. Who has all these attributes? The Lord! Psalm 24:8 asks (and answers), "Who is this King of glory? The LORD strong and mighty, the LORD mighty in battle." And Psalm 62:11 proclaims, "Power belongs to God."

Scripture tells us that God not only has His own power and strength, but He's given that same power to us. He enables us to have energy when we tap into His. David says to God in Psalm 31:4, "You are my strength." And again in Psalm 27:1, "The LORD is my light and my salvation; whom shall I fear? The LORD is the strength of my life; of whom shall I be afraid?" What great verses! What comforting verses! God gives us all the energy we need.

In Isaiah 40:29 we read, "He gives power to the weak, and to those who have no might He increases strength." When I'm exhausted and fall into bed at night, I often think I'll never get up the next morning because I'm utterly played out. Or when I have no more strength to take care of a need or do the things that have been assigned to me, I have to force myself to remember my strength comes from God, not from inside me. There's a vast difference.

Look at this from the last few verses in Isaiah 40: "God doesn't come and go. God *lasts*. He's Creator of all you can see or imagine. He doesn't get tired out, doesn't pause to catch his breath. And he knows *everything*, inside and out. He energizes those who get tired, gives fresh strength to dropouts. For even young people tire and drop out, young folk in their prime stumble and fall. But those who wait upon GOD get fresh strength" (vv. 28–31 MSG).

I've looked at these verses hundreds of times, and they never failed to lift my spirits when I was worn out. The interesting thing is that strength doesn't come from exercise; Isaiah 40 tells us that strength comes from waiting on God. Tomorrow is another day, and God energizes us for it . . . no matter our age. Every day that I get older, those verses bring more comfort.

Be a Steward of Your Money

Then there's the commodity of *money*! Ahh, money. Here's one of the biggest problems in life: how to handle money. How do we master the stewardship of money without becoming its slave? In many ways, money is harder to manage than either time or energy. The first two are God-made commodities, but money is man-made. Maybe that's why it's so hard to manage. But it is barter about which God requires careful accountability, just as He does with our time and energy.

In 1 Timothy 6, the apostle Paul talks about money, cautioning all of us not to get hung up on it. Interestingly, we can be happy about many things in life—our families, jobs, friends, hobbies, leisure—but if we are sidetracked by money, we'll never learn contentment. Ever! In verse 10, Paul writes, "the love of money is a root of all kinds of evil." That's a huge statement. We can self-destruct in no time if money is the ultimate goal. One paraphrase to that verse reads, "Some lose their footing in the faith completely and live to regret it bitterly ever after" (MSG). Be careful with money . . . it's a predator in sheep's clothing. Learn to hold it loosely, remembering it's a gift from God; and like everything else, it belongs to Him. It's only on loan to us.

The second thing I want to mention is that money is an incomparable tool in the hands of someone with a generous heart. It's the avenue of help for people who are less fortunate than we. When properly used, money can offer the poor self-respect, the student an opportunity for more education, the missionary a wage, the victim of tragedy a new start, philanthropic organizations a way to thrive, the abused a reason to get up and keep going . . . on and on.

All of this has to do with the recognition that money is a gift from God. When He places it in the hands of a cheerful giver, the world can change for the better. But it all starts with stewardship—knowing how to hold money loosely and spend it wisely.

In 1993, I began to get very serious about the use of money. I had worked for years and years, making a steady, dependable income. But I hadn't been really serious about managing it. I knew good stewardship principles from my father, but my application hadn't always reflected those principles. So, when 1993 came along, I decided to tap into what I knew was the right thing to do and start over with management principles that work. In January, I wrote down twelve resolutions for the year (Lists! I always make lists!):

Checklist: before you spend:
1. Tithe off the gross.
2. Live within your means.
3. Take care of what you have.
4. Wear it out.
5. Do it yourself.
6. Anticipate your needs.
7. Research value, quality, durability, and multiple use.
8. Make gifts.
9. Shop less.

10. Buy used.

11. Pay cash.

12. Do without.

In my prayer time, I talked to the Lord about putting all of my life before Him . . . including how I handled money. I wanted very much to honor Him as well as live realistically in the here and now. When tax time came and I unexpectedly had to pay an additional twenty thousand dollars I didn't have, I asked God to specifically show me what to do. Should I rob a bank? Obviously, I needed His guidance.

Fortunately, in 1982 (when I first began writing books and speaking—while I was still employed at Mobil Oil Corporation), I had hired a financial adviser to help me invest my book royalties in the best place . . . he's the man I introduced you to in chapter 1—Carl Camp. And now that I had this whopping tax bill, I asked his advice as well. I needed all the counsel I could get. Since my investments were the only reliable source of getting a wad of money (other than borrowing it from a lending institution), he encouraged me to withdraw from my investments (with a penalty of course), and pay the tax bill with that. But I didn't go back from my resolve to keep the checklist. I just tightened my belt, went on a "money diet" (as my friend Mary Graham calls it), and moved ahead. It was a very tight year.

But I learned some things about spending and tithing I could not have learned any other way. And frankly, I enjoyed the challenge. I could feel myself growing stronger in this very important area. I'm grateful for that year, because it was a turning point in handling financial responsibility.

I began to decrease my personal debt by using my checklist. I wrote down all my expenditures, keeping very close track of every penny I spent. Some things I had wanted, I didn't buy; and other things, I bought only when I had the cash. I applied the wise counsel of a mentor from years before: "If the joy of having something is greater than the pain of paying it off, buy it." The onus of responsibility lay in my lap when I applied that. How badly do I want it? Will the having of it bring the joy I'm hoping for? How long will it take me to pay it off? Is it worth the pain each month to go into debt? That axiom worked for me beautifully (and still does). It wasn't easy, but by being careful about debts I had to incur, my spending leveled out. It took several years to come full circle, but it worked.

The next year, I took out a thirty-year loan and bought my first house, at age sixty-one. I made a down payment from the savings account my financial adviser had told me to start seven years before and I moved to Palm Desert, California, to live in my brand-new little condo.

Two years after moving there, the Lord opened the door

for me to start working with Women of Faith. I had *no idea* that was in store. Who knows the future? But I accepted the challenge and began this wonderful journey that is now in its eleventh year. That work enabled me to pay off that condo in nine years (twenty-one years early).

There was not one day I regretted buying that property. I loved my little house! It was a gift from God, and I knew it. I relished it and fully enjoyed His provision. After living there for exactly ten years, I decided to move back to Texas, build a home, and live out the rest of my days in my home state. I found a piece of property I liked and a wonderful, godly, Christian builder and began to put down stakes. At that time I'd saved enough money to make a sizeable down payment, take out another thirty-year loan, and start the next phase of my life. My tithe had grown, my investments had grown, my savings had grown, and my spending was completely under control. God did it!

Oh, and not only did I move—but nine months after that, I paid off this house and now I'm totally debt free. Only God!

I tell you this because I'm such a strong believer that if we get our finances right, other things will fall into place. The discipline it takes to bring our spending under control puts everything else in perspective. As Suze Orman says, "How you handle your money is a reflection of how you handle every aspect of your life." One area of life, then another area, then another. On and on. Stewardship begins to work across the board.

Am I rich? In a thousand ways. Do I have everything I want? Not always. Do I have everything I need? All that and then some. Do I think everyone should spend, save, give, and invest exactly as I do? Of course not. The point is, I was burdened about money. God showed me a way to be free. He led, and I followed (even when it was hard!) And now I'm free.

Tithing is another important issue in handling money (maybe the most important), but it too is a matter of taking God at His word. When He says He will meet all our needs . . . He really does mean *all*. In the same year I made the checklist—1993—I was concerned about tithing. Because I'm single, I always wondered, *If I run out of money who will take care of me?* Chuck, my younger brother, encouraged me to start tithing more than 10 percent, saying to me "Anybody can tithe ten percent, Sis. Go for more." (Then he promised if I "ran out," he'd take care of me and I knew he meant it. But he also knew God was my greatest caregiver).

So I started with 11 percent and have moved steadily up a percentage or two each year since then. The basis of giving is that we give because we have been given to, and how can we ever return measure for measure in that? Psalm 112 talks about those with giving spirits as being wealthy. Verse 9 says, "He gives generously to those in need. His deeds will never be forgotten. He shall have influence and honor" (TLB).

And don't forget *investments.* I've read dozens of books on investing money, and one of the best was written in 1994 (the year after I started my money diet), called *Beardstown Ladies' Common-Sense Investment Guide.* It's a delightful story of sixteen women who outperformed mutual funds and professional money managers three to one. With an average age of sixty-three-and-a-half, these charming senior citizens give their financial secrets in the book, along with great recipes and lots of practical, commonsense advice. Their whole idea is to "learn and earn," and oh how they do it! Some of them even tell you what they bought with their investment earnings. It's a charming book full of wit and wisdom.

As I read this book, I compared my rate of return with theirs and learned a lot about what was going on in my own accounts. It was fun reading and a helpful pursuit for me. It caused me to become more and more centered in the field of investing. I even branched out and asked my financial advisers if I could play with some of my money. They gave me a small chunk of change, with which I bought stock in Starbucks, Disney, Borders, and several others . . . and I've had lots of fun watching it rise . . . and fall. I've learned a lot of good investment principles and found joy along the way.

Finally, I encourage you to give money away. Make plans for this in your budget! My dad used to say to me, "You always need a little change in your pocket, honey, so you can help somebody along the way." Good words! This isn't tithed money. It isn't money to spend on your stuff. It isn't investment money or money to save for your own needs. It's money to be used solely to give away.

Last year, I read about a number of small libraries that were going to be closed unless folks stepped up to the plate and got in the game of helping to save them. I loved that idea, so I sent them money. It wasn't money that was supposed to go somewhere else but part of that loose change in my pocket, so to speak. It felt good to be able to do that. I also have a dear friend in California who founded a theater company for children, and when I found out she needed money last summer to help with their program, it was my delight to contribute.

I've given money toward a down payment on a relative's house, helped kids get into college or go on summer mission trips, paid for friends to travel abroad . . . all because God gave me the money, and I wanted to share it. We're not talking about giving away a big amount of cash; we're talking about a heart that wants to serve and make a contribution along the way. I want to be part of that team.

The joy of making money is helping somebody else have an easier or happier life. My philosophy is this: *I may not be able to do everything, but I can certainly do something.* Let your generosity step up to the plate and join the giving team. It's truly great fun and will bless you in ways you never imagined.

I firmly believe we will never get to the place of truly enjoying money until we learn how to manage it well. That was certainly my case. Money was *always* a problem to me until I gave it to God completely and asked Him to control every aspect of it. That's exactly what He did, and then it was as if he gave it all back. As if He said, "Here, Luci. You know what to do with it now. So have fun! There's a lot more where this came from if you need it. But you're already a millionaire in Me."

Being a good steward of your time, energy, and money will change your whole life.

7 Learn Where to Start

I travel every weekend of my life. Or it seems that way. I get on planes for Women of Faith conferences thirty weekends a year, and then there are vacation flights and other trips. All this involves packing and having things at the ready. You wouldn't believe it, but every time I pack a bag, I'm never quite sure what to take. It depends on the weather. It depends on the engagement. It depends on the length of time I'm gone. But it never fails—when I open the suitcase to start packing, I ask myself, "Where do I start?"

This is especially true if I'm going on vacation. I generally like to take a couple of cameras, a journal, and as few clothes as possible. But which cameras, how fancy a journal, and how many clothes? Normally, I make lists and go by them rigidly so I don't fill the luggage with things I don't need but think I will.

When I was younger, I packed way too much even for an overnight trip—small-framed pictures of my favorite friends, scissors and notebooks and notebook paper and rulers, ink, pens and pen points, books, snacks, games, watches, and rings. By comparison, I now take nothing. Of course, the rules of travel have changed since 9/11, and I'd be a fool to carry what I once did even if I could or wanted to, which I don't.

But I love being surrounded by all my stuff in case I need it immediately. It's there. Packing is an art form, and I've mastered it now.

"Start with What You Know"

There are certain things I have to take on every trip, and they never vary. Because I have a deadline to get those things in the bag and out the door, and I have to start somewhere, I first work on the knowns—cosmetics, underwear, medications, pajamas, and night-light (I never travel without a night-light). Then I move from there to clothes, shoes, and accessories, depending on the season, engagement, and destination. It finally comes down to a science. But it's not easy if I don't start with what I know. If I look at the whole picture, I get confused and waste time trying to decide. Starting with what I know (in any dilemma) is helpful and will ultimately get the job done.

Starting points of any endeavor can be debilitating. We don't want to start something because it seems too hard, too involved, and too much work. Whether it's writing a term paper, building a house, saving money, losing weight, or packing for a trip, we don't know where to begin—so we don't. We think, *The odds are I'll never do it anyway, so why start?*

Life's highway is littered with people who had good intentions but never punched the start button. I know a few people like this, and their questions are always the same: "How did you do that?" "How did you get so organized?" "How do you always finish projects?" "How did you plan that far-fetched vacation to that out-of-the-way spot?" The answer to each of these is the same—*start*. Nobody has the key to the outcome, but we all have the key to possibility. Open the door and walk through it.

I live in the first and only house I have ever built and, I'm sure, ever will. It's a once-in-a-lifetime project. When I started, I knew zero about buying a lot and building a house on it. But I punched start, and my desires began to move down the track. I started with what I knew—I called a realtor, hired a builder, began making drawings of what I wanted, talked to the post office about changing my address, wrote letters, sent e-mails, asked questions, and kept going. I started doing what I knew and only that, and when we start there, the unknowns begin to clear up little by little. I acted on an idea and prayer request to God. As Norman Cousins has said, "The wild dream is the first step to reality. It's the direction-finder by which people locate higher goals and discern their highest selves."

We will never get anywhere unless we start. You can quote me on that! If we begin with a feeling or an urge to do something we've never done before, and if we have the confidence and freedom to believe it can be done, then somehow the difficulties attached to it begin to lose their scary power of intimidation. By trusting in God and believing all things are possible with Him, doors to the unknown begin to open; and in time, a sense of certainty sets in. I've had it happen over and over in my life, and building this house is a perfect example. Now the house is finished. I love it, live in it, and have learned from it numerous lessons about God's keeping His word and giving me abundantly more than I could have ever asked or thought.

Start with Forgiveness

About a year ago, I got an e-mail from someone who had attended a Women of Faith conference in Hartford, Connecticut. She told me how encouraged she was by all the speakers and wanted to shout a few times because it felt so good to be there. Then she confessed when she came that weekend, she'd been very burdened by a relationship that had gone awry many years before, but she couldn't forgive the person who had wronged her.

She wrote something like, "Luci, I really hated that woman. But during the first part of the conference, nobody talked about having been hurt or losing hope over a relationship blowup so I kind of thought I was 'off the hook.' I was OK because nobody mentioned my particular hopelessness. Maybe I didn't have to forgive her because that topic never came up. Then YOU spoke about being hurt by a friend of yours for twenty-five years because she had told a lie about you. I couldn't believe it! I sat there, stunned. Here it was, the end of the day, and that was your big point. I couldn't get over it. It's like I was hearing you say, 'I'm talking to you. Listen to me. You don't have to live like this any longer. You can find hope if you want to. Start with a desire to forgive, and you can.' Amazingly, when I heard you, it was the first time in years I wanted to do something to put an end to my rotten attitude. Thank you."

Forgiveness doesn't come by osmosis. And it's not easy. It begins in our will and moves through our body as we take steps to change things. It's humbling to forgive those who hurt us because there's something in us that wants them to suffer. But those feelings rob us of all the freedom that's possible to enjoy through Christ. And freedom won't come until we *start with forgiveness*.

I so admired the woman who wrote me—not only because telling me that story took courage and transparency, but because making amends after all those years took a fresh start in her life. She had admitted in her spirit that she needed to be forgiving, but she didn't stop there. She took steps to change her attitude and behavior.

Start with a Grateful Heart

Another dilemma in which I often find myself is being cranky or complaining. Something doesn't go my way or come down the pike the way I want it to, so I gripe. It can be any number of things that irritate me—delayed flights, being put on hold, or having to wait in line. Traffic jams. Interruptions. People who don't keep their word. You name it! (You have your own list, don't you?)

At times like these when I'm tempted to gripe, I have to start talking to myself. And when I come to my senses, this is what I say: "Luci, if you can't be content in this moment of inconvenience, be content that it's not worse. Shut up and count your blessings."

But there are times I can't pull myself out of that morass until I *start with a grateful heart*. Our constant attitude should be gratitude. But it seems to be the rarest of virtues. God has given us thousands of reasons to celebrate life every day, even in the worst of times, if we just open our eyes, live in the moment, take in the beauty, and see the possibilities. It's been said, "The worst moment for the atheist is when he feels grateful and has no one to thank."

One of the reasons Thanksgiving is my favorite holiday is that it requires nothing of us but a heart of gratitude. It isn't what we have in our pocket that counts; it's what we have in our hearts when we come to that gathering with family, friends, and neighbors. At Christmas, there are too many trappings for my taste—obligations, gifts to buy, houses to decorate, cards to send . . . so many deadlines. But Thanksgiving is a gift all its own, wrapped in laughter, singing, fellowship, games, good food, and sweet sharing. Some of the best memories of my parents, brothers, and friends are built around that holiday.

For those of you out there who live alone, I can also tell you from experience that it's important to have a grateful heart about living by yourself. And in many ways, each one of us is essentially alone. We "exist within our own unique epidermal envelope as a separate thing," Thomas Wolfe once wrote. But that can be a wonderful thing.

Learn Where to Start

Living alone has taught me not only to tolerate solitude but revel in it. I've learned to confront my fears and become comfortable with my inner self. In fact, solitude isn't a luxury but a requirement for me now. It gives me good mental health. When I'm alone, I process life's experiences, think through choices, replenish my energy, and face myself without other distractions. Sometimes that's pleasant; sometimes it's not. But it's never without value.

The German psychologist Erich Fromm believes our ability to love others is predicated upon whether or not we can enjoy time alone. He says if we're not comfortable with our own company, we'll never be able to love anybody else out of desire rather than need. That's an enormous thought! And I agree. So a heart of gratitude leads us down many avenues that enhance personal growth and teach us to celebrate life just as it is, without balloons, streamers, confetti, and horns blowing. The fact that we're alive is the celebration. When I look at life this way, it negates all my griping and crankiness. It puts it in its place. After all, the best of human freedoms is the ability to choose my own attitude in any set of circumstances. I have the right as a human being to decide what I feel, how I live, and what I am inside. And I choose gratitude!

Start with Expediency

Another hurdle is learning how to incorporate what is immediately advantageous. It's doing those things in life that are practical, prudent, or suitable for the moment. The doing of them may not be long-term, but they have the best immediate end in view. They're the methods we employ along life's way to make life work better and easier for us. These little temporary enterprises are born out of our desire to achieve a particular goal. To get to that goal, we *start with expediency*.

When I was in my twenties and thirties, for example, I had four jobs. I worked for Mobil Oil Corporation as a draftsman-artist, from which I drew a regular monthly salary. Additionally, every fall, I sang as a chorister in the Dallas Civic Opera, from which I drew paychecks during the four-month opera season. I was also the soloist for a Methodist church across town, from which I drew a check for those Sundays I sang for their service. And finally, I did drafting work in my home for a man who was beginning his own business and needed help from a qualified artist. My reason for all those jobs, obviously, was to have more income for personal goals I had set for myself during that time. The first job lasted thirty years, and I retired from it in 1987. Singing with the opera lasted fifteen years, and every fall it was a wonderful, fun diversion that lasted until I moved to another state. And the final two jobs were done here and there . . .a few months at a time for friends of mine just to help them out in their need and make a little "mad money" to jingle in my pocket.

All but the first job were jobs of expediency. They were short-term with an end view in mind. I would never work like that today. My financial needs have changed, and I don't have the energy to do any more than I'm doing. I'm beyond the age of holding down four jobs simultaneously. But they served a very important purpose and helped set in motion a good savings program that was the foundation for the money I'll live off of when I really do retire . . . if ever!

I do other things now for expediency's sake. Because of my very, very busy schedule with Women of Faith, I try to think of everything I can to save time: have my cleaning picked up and delivered, eat out more than I cook, leave certain bags packed all the time instead of unpacking between conferences, have a personal shopper and decorator, buy gifts instead of making them, write more e-mail than snail mail, and have a pickup service drive me to the airport instead of taking my own car. I can think of twenty things I do every day, week, and month that enable me to reach my goals. But five years from now, I may do none of them. They serve their purpose now, and now is where I live and have to get the job done. You get my point!

Everything has a shelf life, my friends. There's a time to live and a time to die. Every cause has not only an effect but a means to be accomplished. That's what I'm talking about with expediency. When we think like that, we get a lot done; and slowly, slowly, our goals are realized. For some of us it will mean hiring a nanny or baby-sitter, having a secretary, using a maid service to clean our houses, or engaging an assistant to keep us on track. Whatever it takes for expediency's sake seems to be the wise way for the busy person to get things finished. Sometimes, we simply have to get the responsibility off ourselves.

My computer has a funny little quirk: it won't start unless I punch the start button twice. It's been that way since the first day it was up and running. I've had tech people work on it, and it still has the quirk. So I accept it as part of its idiosyncrasies. I've learned what it takes to get the thing started, and that's what I do. It's as simple as that.

Some of our lives are the same way. We have a hard time getting off the start line. I'm suggesting you do what it takes to make your life work. Study your habits and patterns. See what's best for you. Keep pressing ahead, and punch whatever buttons will get you up and running. Once you learn that and keep doing it, many of your battles will be over.

8 Learn When to Stop

Knowing when to stop is one of the hardest exercises in the world. I'm seventy-three and still trying to learn it. And I mean stopping for any reason. Not just knowing when to retire—which seems logical in the fulfillment of a long working career—but knowing when to stop driving a car, stop traveling abroad, stop packing to move, stop trimming trees, or stop volunteering at church. I can name any number of things we do in our everyday lives that may have a stopping point, but when is that? The answer differs with each person.

Nobody can dictate when you have to stop doing something. Sometimes God puts on the brakes with health problems or other life circumstances, but apart from those, we rarely know the best time to stop doing something. How can we know for sure where the stopping point is in any activity? When is the best time to say no? What is the right moment to transition from one thing to another?

There is no definitive answer to these questions—and don't let anybody tell you there is. What might work for me might not work for you. And since I've tried twice to retire and it hasn't stuck, I'm not a good one to advise others on a proper stopping point. My father worked every day until well into his eighties, and that was long after retiring from his "last" job. I wrote my first book at fifty, traveled all over the world at sixty, and built my first house at seventy, so what will I be doing at eighty? Who knows? But unless I'm forced to, I have no intention of stopping.

Sometimes I feel like my life has just started because finally, *finally* I've learned how to truly live—how to enjoy a life that's balanced and fulfilled. I've figured out a few things that help me cope with the demands and vicissitudes of daily living. No one ever arrives, of course, but I'm a lot further along than I once was. I only wish I had known a long time ago about what I'm writing in this chapter. I wish someone had told a much younger me the best way to grow old, but they didn't. Maybe they didn't know either. Perhaps we learn the secret of aging by living fully right up to the edge of dying.

I read about women like Julia Child, who was ninety-two when she died. Until the very end of her life, she contributed to the culinary world more than any other person her age. She also taught us to savor life to the fullest. She once said, "A passionate interest in what you do is the secret of enjoying life, perhaps the secret of long life, whether it is helping old people or children or making cheese or growing earthworms."

May Sarton wrote in her journal, *At Seventy*, "I am a far more complete and richer person than I was at twenty-five, when ambition and personal conflicts were paramount and there was a surface of sophistication that was not true of the person inside."[1] Or Grandma Moses—she lived 101 years, and at age 100 she gave a birthday party for herself and danced a jig.

One of my friends at Women of Faith has an eighty-one-year-old grandmother who got a marriage proposal from her ninety-one-year-old "boyfriend." She can't decide whether or not to marry him . . . she wants to think about it. In the meantime, my friend suggested she hurry up before she's too old to be a flower girl. Don't you just *love* that?

In the mid-1990s, I read a delightful book called *Having Our Say: The Delany Sisters' First 100 Years*.[2] It was by two black sisters—Sarah, 103, and Bessie, 101. When Bessie was growing up, she always said she'd like to be as old as Moses (who lived to be 120), and she almost made it. When her sister said that, Sarah told her she herself would have to live to be 122, so she could take care of her in her old age. They both claim they never thought anybody would be interested in hearing what "two old Negro women" had to say about life. But we're very interested in what they have to say, because life was always full of surprises to them and they made the most of every day. That's what we all want. We want to grow old like that. Who says we can't?

King David asked of the Lord in the Psalm 90, "We live for seventy years or so (with luck we might make it to eighty), and what do we have to show for it? Trouble. Toil and trouble and a marker in the graveyard. . . . Oh! Teach us to live well! Teach us to live wisely and well!" (vv. 10, 12 MSG).

When I was in college, I had an elderly friend whom I loved dearly. Her name was Edna, and she was an unforgettable example of one who lived wisely and well. I was twenty, and she was eighty—a sixty-year age difference between us. But I never felt that difference when we were together—we were *girlfriends*. Edna's little home was a couple of blocks from the campus, and many Sundays I went with her daughter to visit Edna. Those were my favorite Sundays: church, lunch, Edna . . . in that order. She was the youngest old person I've ever known!

She loved opera and classical music, which rang out all over the house and into her yard, filled with hundreds of flowers in neat little beds running alongside a trimmed, manicured lawn. As the music played, she often sang along . . . a bit off-key, but who cared? She loved it, and everybody who stepped on that lawn did too.

Edna's house was crammed with books, in every corner—on the floor, the bed, the counter, the chairs. I'd talk with her about the ones she especially liked, and every now and then she'd break into poetry, quoting verse after verse. She read her books over and over and often said about a certain volume, "That one is as old as I am. I've read it four times."

Edna never stopped learning and growing. She memorized the Psalms while she washed dishes. She painted her own bathroom and made her own curtains. She shopped and cooked and cleaned and gardened. I'm sure she got tired and often needed help, but she never quit living or sharing her life with others. And she never complained.

The other day when I was roaming around in my own library, putting away books I'd been reading, I thought about Edna, wishing she could come over for tea. In part, because I wanted to show her my library and share my home with her, but mostly because I wanted to thank her for the legacy she passed on to me and never knew it. She's one of my sweetest memories of college days.

Scripture teaches us to number our days and to apply our hearts unto wisdom. It also says even though we're "wasting away" on the outside, we are being renewed inwardly day by day. Those two verses say a lot about the aging process. It's a lifelong journey that has neither a clear beginning nor clear ending. But there are signs along the way that one's body is changing. We see our hair turning gray. Wrinkles show up in our faces as they become seasoned and worn with time. We do things more slowly and deliberately. Our skeletal frame and skin seems to be lower to the ground, and what isn't lower or in need of repair has already fallen off! These are the signs of the outside wasting away.

But it's the inside that's being renewed daily. And *that's* what we want to concentrate on. It's those things inside we must learn to stop for. This is the secret of happy aging. Although obvious signs of physical changes are known to all of us, life's journey takes us beyond the obvious. It reaches inside and teaches us lessons we can only learn with our mind, spirit, and heart. The outward appearance becomes secondary to a far more endearing beauty and strength. The physical appearance of youth may be gone, but the capacity to love, experience, enjoy, share, and create grow even stronger. Therefore, these are the areas where we must learn to stop and ponder.

Stop to Enjoy Reflection

I counted my journals today. There are fifty-four. Some are travel journals from different trips and excursions through the years, but most are daily journals in which I've recorded activities, thoughts, ponderings, and concerns. By writing them, I've wanted to leave a trace that I've crossed life's threshold and hopefully made a difference to somebody. There are numerous times I've reread those journals and thought about the moment this or that was written. I've pondered stories of my past. I've cried over pictures of those I loved who are no longer with me here on earth. I've laughed over antics by which my friends made me happy. I've read scriptures that meant something very meaningful to me at a particular time. I've remembered how I felt in an embarrassing moment or time of deep sadness. I've spent *hours* reflecting in those pages, and I'm the richer for it. There are countless snapshots of my daily life over the years.

To *reflect* is to trace the route that a particular memory first took through the senses. In my mind's eye I see the person, hear his voice, feel his touch, and recall the conversation I wrote about.

If I don't keep a journal, my life is hidden from myself—and I don't want that. I don't want to forget, and I know I will if I've not written some sort of daily log. I want to be able to look back and not lose the memory of what I did years before. I want to remember how I came to a certain decision, why I developed certain patterns, and when I got in touch with certain feelings about what was bothering me.

Did you know Leonardo da Vinci kept journals for forty years? In the morning, he recorded dreams. In the afternoon, he jotted notes or ideas. In the evening, he wrote down passages he had read. And look what his reflections produced! I don't think for a minute that my journals will ever come close to those of Leonardo da Vinci's, and they don't need to. I'm writing them for me, so I can recall facts and feelings without wondering about the details of what happened—or worse, forgetting them altogether.

There's more than one meaning of the term *reflection*. I'm using it here to mean thinking quietly and calmly . . . to be thoughtful, to look back in meditation. It also means an image given back by a reflecting surface. In many ways, that's what the pages of a journal do: they mirror your past back to you. I think that's interesting because it gives those pages additional value.

I could talk all day about the benefits of keeping a journal, but that may not work for everyone. Primarily, I'm suggesting we think back, remember, be still and thoughtful about where we've come from, what you've come through, and why it's important.

Stop to Find Pleasure

Pleasure has many forms: beauty, laughter, solace, companionship, solitude, love. Even giftedness. It can be playful, sensual, enriching, or frivolous. Even worshipful. Some-times when I'm praying, I thank the Lord for the pleasure of His company. I love knowing He is with me, that He cares about me and He makes my heart feel grateful, content, and full. All of those thoughts bring me pleasure, and I want Him to know that from my heart. I want to tell Him.

What is your most pleasant feeling? Mine is relief. I love that feeling more than any other. When I'm hungry, eating brings relief. When I'm tired, sleep gives relief. When I'm lonely, companionship gives relief. When I'm standing in a long line wearing bad shoes, even an inadequate place to sit feels wonderful. Anything uncomfortable that finds relief gives the feeling of pleasure. And nothing on this earth is more wonderful than something that relieves my soul. This is what I'm talking about. Someone has said,

"Work is the meat of life; pleasure is the dessert." Pleasure is a wonderful, delightful, enjoyable feeling, and I believe we should stop for it in life. It makes our time on this earth sweeter and easier to bear.

Stop to Be Creative

The longer I live, the more I appreciate the fruits of creativity. In the words of Rollo May, "Creativity keeps us fresh." He uses the word "fresh" instead of "young" because he doesn't see young as a desirable state. Neither do I.

I've often said if someone offered me a million dollars to go through my twenties again, they could keep their money. No way! Those were my hardest years. Trying to find my way through the morass of individuation almost killed me. Determining who I was, what I thought, and what I wanted to do with my life felt like a constant battle. Now that I've come out on the other side, I wouldn't repeat those years for any amount of money—nor would I sell them for any amount. They're under my belt, and in many ways, going through them taught me some of life's most valuable lessons. Even if it was nothing more than, "I'll never do *that* again."

Being creative is to find your own voice inside yourself, to identify your own ideas and aspirations. It means singing the song that's in your heart, to your own melody. You're the only one who can hear it, because it's coming to you from God. If you look at this song with your intellect, it goes away because it doesn't respond to your mind; it responds to your heart. The mind turns it cold, and it quits singing. These are the pinnacles of experience that caused the great masters of art to produce what they did. These personal moments give the greatest happiness and greatest wisdom.

Consider Henri Matisse, the famous French artist. His entire life was dedicated to painting in oils. We've all seen his work and marveled at his genius. All his subjects—flowers, landscapes, women, still-life compositions—display his fascination with color and design.

When he was an old man, Matisse became very ill and was confined to a wheelchair or his bed. Because of that, he had time to think and reflect. (There's our word!) Being detached from his active life, he wrote, "My terrible operation has made a philosopher of me . . . it seems to me now that I am in a second life." Matisse was weak and his strength was diminished, so instead of taking a pen or brush in his hand, he took a pair of scissors . . . something we use every day. He cut out designs and life forms, and with a long pole, stuck them up on the wall around his bedroom, dining room, and studio. He created a whole new world . . . a new way of thinking and looking at art and life. He sang the song that was inside him and found a new, creative voice. His famous cutouts began to express a new beauty in his house-bound life. They were fresh, alive, and charmingly different from anything the art world had ever seen.

Matisse called on all his collective knowledge, wisdom, and love to demonstrate what he felt and saw with his inner eye even though he was old and debilitated. He opened his heart to a new way of thinking, and the result is incredibly beautiful work for all of us to enjoy as long as we live. Near his death, he said, "One must observe a lot. One has only one life, and one is never finished."

I have a framed print of one of his cut-outs on my living room wall; I bought it at the National Gallery of Art in Washington, D.C. It's a great reminder to me that life is still flowing through my veins, and I must continually stop to create what I hear inside my heart. (Incidentally, it's called *The Wine Press*, and the original sold a few years ago for $29 million.

Stop to Evaluate Your Purpose

In today's world, it's very easy to get off track. There are many roads that lead to a dead end even though they feel right at the time. One of the reasons it's such a joy to work for an organization like Women of Faith is because it has far-reaching, definable goals and purposes. This ministry is designed to reach women everywhere—churched, unchurched, believers, unbelievers, Christian, non-Christian, poor, wealthy, all races, all colors, all creeds—with the good news that Christ died for their sins and has made a way for them to know God personally through faith in His Son, Jesus. We do that by telling our stories of how God meets us along life's way and by proclaiming the message of God's love, forgiveness, and grace. That is our ultimate purpose and our largest concern.

Inevitably, because we are all in the human condition, it's somewhat easy to get off that target. Commercialism or religious jargon or political issues can sidetrack us. Fortunately, the Women of Faith organization has a president (Mary Graham) who is centered on and governed by our basic mission, so she keeps us on point—in our messages, music, partnerships, and behavior. I'm glad. It enables me to reevaluate and define my purpose at any given moment in my work.

In our private lives, we need to do the same. How are we spending our time, energy, and money? Is it in line with our God-given purpose in life? If so, go for it. If not, stop and look at what needs to be changed.

Stop to Gain Eternal Perspective

Everything has a shelf life. There will come a day when my life will end as I know it. Do I have a will or a living trust? Are the bills paid? Do I owe anybody money? Have I done the best I could? All these are little "housekeeping" duties. As sure as night will come, so will my death. Am I ready for that? Sometimes I feel like Woody Allen, who said, "I don't mind death; I just don't want to be there when it happens." Me neither.

I know for a fact where I will go when I die, and I believe God's Word on that subject is absolutely true. Nevertheless, having no testimony from one who has gone before and come back to report . . . I wonder about some things. Will anything about death hurt? Will I go right into the throne room with Jesus? Will I see people right away who have gone before? What age will I be when I get there?

I don't know any of those things for sure, and I'm curious about them. But I do know I'm going to heaven, and I'm ready. It's not on my to-do list, because it's already done. I'm outta here when the trumpet sounds.

In short, I'd like to live forever. And I will—not on this earth, of course, but in heaven. Until then, I want to be

Life! Celebrate It

looking for new possibilities, trying new things, and enjoying new friends, ideas, and accomplishments. No matter how many years I live on this earth, my heart will never be old.

part three

Laugh!

9 Laugh with Life

Humor punctuated my grandmother's life. Whether her words ended in a period, comma, semicolon, question mark, or exclamation point, laughter was her punctuation of choice. She died in her eighties, which was way too soon for me, because her life was a guiding light of joy. I miss her still.

As a young woman rearing four children, my grandmother laughed with life and taught her kids to do the same. When my brothers and I were youngsters, my mother often treated us to stories about her own childhood with "Momo" (that's what we called my grandmother), and without exception, laughter was part of the telling. Even in sadness or difficulty, Momo found moments of comedy.

For example, one Sunday night during church, my grandfather was called out of the service to go with a police officer to the scene of a car accident involving several vehicles on the outskirts of their little Texas town, El Campo. Being a justice of the peace, Granddaddy often dealt with matters of law or public decorum regarding local citizens, most of whom he knew personally. Momo couldn't bear not knowing what happened, who was involved, whether anyone was hurt, the location of the pileup, and everything involved with the accident, but she wasn't asked to go with them.

Being hopelessly nosy, the minute church was over, Momo grabbed the children, marched out to the family car, asked a friend to drive her (she never drove a day in her life), and headed straight for the scene of the accident. This was in the early 1920s, so car ownership was more or less at a premium. Even the smallest fender bender was front-page news. All the way there, Momo was coming up with different scenarios, trying to figure out what happened, putting together in her mind various pictures of what it looked like, all of which were based on her own imagination.

The truth was, Momo knew nothing about cars. She didn't know make or model or year or any information of value. All she knew was color. You'd ask her, "What kind of a car does Mr. Grant drive?" and she'd answer, "Blue."

When they pulled up to an area where lights were flashing and police cars had gathered, it was indeed a mess. Four cars had smashed together on a dirt road, two of which had overturned and landed in an open field. Momo asked to be let out immediately so she could find out what happened and whether anyone was seriously hurt.

Stepping out, she headed straight into the fray as her friend drove the car with her kids to the other side of the pileup to get out of the way of vehicles arriving. After looking around awhile and learning that no one was seriously hurt, Momo walked through the wreck and came to the very car in which she had arrived. Then she leaned in the window and in all seriousness asked, "Can you folks tell me what happened here tonight?"

Her kids nearly died laughing and said, "Mother, get in the car. It's *us*." To the sound of raucous shrieking, she crawled in the backseat, and the car literally shook with laughter. I never learned whether or not anyone was hurt that night. All we ever heard was that it was one more story about Momo's laughing life . . . and herself.

I always marveled at Momo's ability to punctuate situations with laughter that could be otherwise heartbreaking. She often said, "A day is wasted unless we fall over in a heap laughing." I can hear her words in my head now.

Momo came to see our family often when we lived in Houston, because El Campo was only an hour or so away.

Since she didn't drive and Granddaddy was working, she'd hop on a Greyhound bus and be on her way.

One particular weekend, she came to attend a school event where one of my brothers was being featured in a play. I don't recall the play or his part, but I do remember Momo's words as she was going home the next evening. As she was getting on the bus to leave, she paused for just a second, turned around, and commented, "This weekend was kind of a waste, don't you think? We didn't laugh enough. What's wrong with us?"

That outlook on life defined my grandmother. Sometimes nowadays when life goes too fast and I'm caught up in my own speed, unable or unwilling to notice anything funny, I remember what she said back then and say to myself, "What's wrong with me? I haven't laughed today."

Granted, not everyone has my grandmother's temperament. By nature, Momo was carefree and happy—and mischievous. Mother told me when she was dating Daddy, my grandfather wasn't all that eager for her to go out with him because he'd been divorced. Even though he was in Granddaddy's employ and very highly respected, Granddaddy wondered what his church friends would think about his daughter dating a divorced man. (Remember, this was back in 1930.)

But Momo was crazy about my dad and had worked

out a plan to get around that problem. Carefully and with an ulterior motive, she engaged Granddaddy in conversation in the back of the house while Daddy came in the front, fetched Mother and took her out for a little drive. No harm done. One hour later, Mother was back, Daddy was gone, Momo was gleeful, and Granddaddy was none the worse for wear.

There's more than one way to boil an egg.

And speaking of eggs, Momo wrote a note to her kids once that read, "Gone next door to borrow an egg." My mother kept that note for years. When I asked her why she kept it, Mother said, "Because she was gone so long we think she probably went off to fly a kite and knew we'd want to come with her if she told us. She did that sort of thing, you know. She was full of mischief and fun."

"But did she come back with the egg?" I asked.

"Oh yeah." Mother grinned. "But it was at least an hour later."

I'm so much like Momo! I'm carefree, cheerful, mischievous, and happy by nature. It helps to be that way when things are tough, because sometimes things just aren't funny. You're having a rotten day, and laughter is the last thing on your mind. I've been there. I know that feeling very well. So what do I do? Let me suggest what works for me.

Shift the Weight

Before we can overcome life's maddening battles and get on with having fun, we must understand one weighty principle: life is difficult. Throughout the pages of God's Word, we read over and over that we will experience tribulation, heartache, testing, and difficulty in this life. No matter who you are, that fact will never change this side of heaven. Even if you stick your head in the sand, hard times will definitely come.

With that as a given, it's our responsibility to be content and cheerful anyway. How? For one thing, by shifting the weight off yourself and onto God. When we give to Him what is weighing us down, He lifts it off our shoulders and enables us to stand up and go on. In spite of the feelings that come with problems, we'll be given the energy to carry on. But we have to do that first, or the weight will be too heavy to keep going forward. We want to sit down. Or worse, we want to die.

My grandmother was no saint, but she refused to get buried under the load of care she had as a mother, a wife, a church member, a grandmother, and a human being. Every one of those callings has problems attached to it. So how did she do it? She had her own *querencia*. (It sounds like the word *Corinthian*, only with "ah" on the end.)

In Spanish, this word means a favorite and frequent place of rest for wild beasts. In bullfighting, for example, it was that small area in the bullring, maybe fifty feet square, in which the fighting bull fancies himself as completely safe and relaxed. I've seen lions do this in Africa. They find their *querencia* under trees or near old, rotting logs where there's shade. Life is still hard, and the animals are still ferocious and unpredictable, but they've found just the right spot to spread out and quit battling with the inevitable for a while.

By the same token, we human beings have an undefined place of peace that God offers to us, and we seek it out instinctively. By shifting the weight of tough stuff off our shoulders onto God's, we find that place to relax. It's still a jungle out there, but we unconsciously find that quiet place—our *querencia*—where we stop grinding out life's maddening pace for a few minutes. This spot is inside us, and God makes it available so we can pause and catch our breath. Laugh. Sing. Think. Pray. Everyday rhythms and patterns of life keep going, but we're not going with them. We're listening to the beat of a different drum.

This is what Isaiah was talking about in his book: "He energizes those who get tired, gives fresh strength to dropouts. For even young people tire and drop out, young folk in their prime stumble and fall. But those who wait upon GOD get fresh strength. They spread their wings and soar like eagles, they run and don't get tired, they walk and don't lag behind" (40:29–30 MSG).

Find your own *querencia* and go there. If you are over-whelmed by a problem that seems impossible to solve, don't! Quit trying to solve it. At least for right now. Go to your *querencia*. Like Momo, shift the weight of your problems to God, and the rest of your life and your family will be the richer for it.

Clear Your Head

I knew a guy who raised pigeons. He made his living that way, breeding and raising these little plump, fast-flying birds with small heads and low, crooning voices. He must have had two hundred pigeons at a time for sale.

It's my understanding that tending pigeons is no picnic. They're messy and noisy and leave trails of seeds and grain everywhere they go. Not to mention their excrement! But this guy loved those birds, and he always kept their cages clean and tidy. I asked him what the magic was between him and pigeons. "They make me laugh," he said. "And they clear my head."

"What do you mean?" I asked.

"Well, first of all, they stand on each other and stomp

around like they're dancing together to their own little tune. It's just funny. And when I watch their little dance, it takes my mind off my own problems."

I have to admit, I know some pretty funny birds myself! There's one in Africa called the crowned lapwing, with gorgeous markings and long, orange spindly legs. They look like they're wearing high heels. Normally, these birds stand and stare at life, but when they feel threatened, they go insane and fly about, warning all the other birds and mammals in the vicinity that something's up. They're a scream to watch, especially when *they're* screaming!

And there's the long-tailed willow, which flies straight up in the air (as if shot out of a cannon), and then dives down again and, with its long, feathered tail, beats the high grass, creating a nest on the ground with a small fancy, tidy, side entrance. Ingenious. And comical.

I could go on, but I'll quit with this last bird story. A couple of years ago, Mary Graham, Nicole Johnson, and I went to Antarctica on a cruise with a whole boatload of "birders." (We used to call them bird-watchers in my younger days, but I've learned better.)

Prior to departure, the three of us were playing Scrabble one night, and Nicole used the word *bloater*, which I questioned. She swore it was a bona fide word, so I let her get by with it. (We had no dictionary for verification.) We laughed about "bloater" and teasingly called each other that loving name after meals when we were too full to waddle or when we asked each other, "Does this parka make my butt look big?"

But there came the night onboard the ship when the three of us were seated at a table in which *all* the other people were birders, including the former president of the Audubon Society and his wife. Oh my. What now? He was a lovely person, as was she. When he asked if I was a birder, I searched my mind quickly for a sweet way to say, "Heavens, no; I hardly know anything about birds"—but instead, what came out was, "No, I'm a bloater." Nicole and Mary laughed their heads off, and after a thorough explanation, this wonderful man threw his head back and did the same. Needless to say, he became our hero throughout the trip, and we learned many things about birds and their habits from him and his wife. They were charming, fun-loving people with whom we exchanged crazy comments for ten days.

Life! It can be pretty funny. Maddening? Sometimes. Overwhelming? Of course. But funny? Absolutely.

I strongly suggest that when you feel overwhelmed, look for ways to clear your head. When you're feeling pressure in your job, find a little something funny to wipe out the cobwebs. When you're trying to figure out your flailing finances, take a quick side trip to your *querencia*. It won't bring your checkbook into balance, but it might do just that for you.

Come to Pass

If shifting the weight and clearing your head fail to provide a measure of relief, then remember this: whatever difficulty you're facing today has only come to pass. You know how great literature as well as Scripture often reads, "And it *came to pass* . . ."? That's what I'm talking about. Whatever your burden at the moment, you can be sure that it, too, will pass. One day, it will be no more!

The word *pass* is a wonderful word. In my dictionary, it has twelve different meanings. And while each is interesting, and most of us have used the word in all its meanings at one time or another, it's the first definition to which I refer here: "to proceed; to go away; to depart."

Whatever burden you're facing at the moment *will* depart. It's just a matter of time. It came to pass, and it will. But it's between those two moving targets—*came* and *pass*—that we need to look for humor, isn't it? Some things that come are better than we could ever hope for, while others are life-shatteringly hard.

One of my funniest friends has a burden beyond measure

to bear. Her husband was recently diagnosed with an inoperable brain tumor, and the prognosis is bleak. Nevertheless, my friend, from whom I receive regular updates, continues to be articulate, warm, charming, balanced, and funny. As a Christian, she has put her faith in God, who is her strength and shield in this matter with her husband.

When I watch her, what I see and hear is remarkable, to say the least. In the midst of tragedy and sorrow, she can still be downright *funny*! How? Because she knows this time of trial is going to pass. She may not get the answer out of it she wants, but she hasn't given up hope, and she hasn't forfeited her sense of humor. She's claiming verses like this one, again from our old friend, the prophet Isaiah: "Don't be afraid, I've redeemed you. I've called your name. You're mine. When you're in over your head, I'll be there with you. When you're in rough waters, you will not go down. When you're between a rock and a hard place, it won't be a dead end—because I am GOD, your personal God, the Holy of Israel, your Savior" (43:1–3 MSG).

My friend believes that and hangs on to it. This scripture is interesting, because the New International Version of that same passage says, "When you *pass through* the waters, I will be with you" (emphasis mine). Notice that my friend is *passing through* her husband's illness. Her heartache won't last forever, and the pain she's enduring will pass. It has come to do just that!

Remember, we'll never get out of this life without facing big problems or having our hearts broken. It's not possible, so don't spend time trying to reason it out otherwise. Don't wait for a utopia that doesn't exist.

When we accept the inevitability of trials and suffering and accept their mandate for living fully wherever we are and whatever we're doing, a great part of the battle has already been won by Someone who is much stronger and braver than we. And we belong to Him. He punctuates our life with laughter and joy.

10 Laugh with Others

I just talked with my dear friend Marilyn Meberg. "How ya doin'?" I asked. Without hesitation, she responded, "I'm perfectly content—as content, that is, as one can be while living in an imperfect world and in a body whose days are numbered." Whoa! I laughed out loud. In two seconds, she answered my question, gave me something to think about, stated the dilemma of the human race, and tickled my funny bone. No one I know does that as well as Marilyn. It's her quirky wit.

Marilyn and I met in 1973, and we've been laughing with each other ever since. Ours is a delightful, satisfying friendship that has been tested by fire, fed by God's Spirit,

117

enlightened by ideas, and enriched by humor. I hadn't known her very long before we were talking about the similarities and differences between marriage and singleness. I was stating some obvious challenges of living alone and said something like, "I don't think married people fully understand loneliness, because they've got a partner."

She shot back, "Oh, Luci, anybody can be lonely. Marriage doesn't preclude loneliness."

I thought for a second, realizing there was truth to that. But for the life of me, I couldn't remember what *preclude* meant. So I casually asked, "Now what does *preclude* mean, Marilyn? I can't remember."

"I don't know, but Rachmaninoff wrote one."

Marilyn's quick wit totally derailed my train of thought, and I forgot everything I was going to say after that. The conversation just stopped while we both laughed and laughed, like two kids.

I love being around people who seem to have nonsense in their veins. They're the ones who erase tension in business meetings, liven up a schoolroom or office discussion, and relieve boredom wherever they go. If you have someone like that in your life, you need to stop right now and thank God, because that person is a beautiful gift straight from heaven. Anne Lamott says, "Nothing gives hope like laughter. It moisturizes the soul." The difficulties of life break down into manageable sizes. It's a "momentary anesthesia of the heart," to quote French philosopher Henri Bergson.

All my "Porch Pals" on the Women of Faith speaking team value a sense of humor as much as I, and each of them has a razor-sharp wit. Their ability to find laughter in life was actually a prerequisite for joining the team. When we first started working for this ministry, we were simply told to "make 'em laugh"—and that's one thing we've enjoyed doing ever since. Of course, we also have to say something of value, but the ability to find humor in tough times and to encourage others to do the same is still high on our priority list.

Interestingly, research shows that laughter itself serves no biological purpose. It's a reflex action, sometimes called a "luxury reflex," unrelated to humanity's struggle for survival. Yet the emotional service it provides can't begin to be measured. According to Proverbs 17:22, laughter is "good medicine" (NIV)—and we've all experienced a healthy dose of that medicine when we didn't even know we were sick. Laughter lifts our spirit and drops the fever. Somehow, it opens the windows to our soul, letting in light and fresh air. A friend of mine used to say, "Laughter is kind of like changing my baby's diaper—it doesn't solve any problems permanently, but it certainly makes things more enjoyable at the moment."

Betting on a Good Laugh

When I moved from Texas to California in 1974, Marilyn and I lived in the same neighborhood (which has been the case most of the thirty-plus years we've been friends). We lived in the LA Basin in a small town called Fullerton. Shortly after my cross-country move, Marilyn asked if Id like to go with her to Palm Springs. "Sure," I said. "I'd love that. Isn't that the place where movie stars are on every corner?"

"I don't know about that, but it's my favorite city in California, and I'd love to introduce it to you."

I was excited. At this point, I had only heard of Palm Springs as a laid-back, casually elegant, always sunny, wealthy resort of the jet set. Now I could check it out for myself. So off we went for our little overnight excursion.

After an afternoon of soaking in our hotel's pool, we dressed and went into town. Window shopping and driving around led us to an Italian restaurant on the main drag called Banducci's. (You might know the place.) It's a nice spot with attractive décor, reasonable prices, and good food. Apparently, many Hollywood stars have been there, because their pictures line the walls. And every picture included a blonde woman whom neither of us recognized as anyone famous. "Who's that gal?" we asked each other as we walked by this gallery of greats.

Quickly seated in a booth, we placed our order; and within minutes, this very woman emerged from the kitchen. Attractive, tall, and smiling, she casually went from table to table, greeting the customers. We agreed she must be the owner, Mrs. Banducci.

There was soft piano music coming from a lounge somewhere behind us, obscured by a partition. *What a lovely evening,* I thought. *I'm enjoying this.* Marilyn interrupted my thoughts when she looked me straight in the eye and asked, "Luci, do you like bets?"

"Yeah! I love bets, Marilyn. All my life I've loved bets but have rarely known others who did, so I usually squelched my little desire. But if you like bets, too, we're going to be very good friends," I said, laughingly. She assured me I had met my match. Then she asked if I wanted to make a bet with her.

"Absolutely. What do you have in mind?"

"Let's guess who that pianist is," she said. "The one in the bar. We can't see him (or her), so let's guess the sex, hair color, and approximate age, and the one who comes the closest wins. OK?"

"Love it," I responded. Then I asked, "What does the winner get?"

Marilyn cocked her head, thought a moment, and then said, "Let's just say she gets her way. Whoever loses has to do whatever the winner wants, no matter what. Does that sound fair?"

"Well, yeah. You mean, if I guess the person, then I win and you have to do what I want?"

"That's right. And by the same token, if I win, you have to do what I want."

"Sounds fair to me." I jumped on this! "I'll go first. This pianist is a woman, about fifty, blonde, and she looks a lot like Mrs. Banducci . . . might even be her sister. You know, the owner gives her sister a job and—"

Marilyn interrupted me. "No way. This is a man. I *know* the touch of a man."

"Oh, shut up, Marilyn."

"Really. But this is no ordinary guy. It's somebody who looks like Buddha—kind of overweight with a plump little body and fat fingers. A fringe of black hair around his head . . ." And on and on she went.

Obviously, our descriptions were totally different. I said, "Hold it right there. I'll go look." When I peeked around the corner of the partition, there sat Buddha. I'm not kidding. Fat guy, fringe of hair, and playing piano beautifully. I was stunned. I muttered something about her having been there before, but she assured me she hadn't.

So here I was, hung out to dry by this ludicrous bet, and Marilyn was going to tell me some wild, harebrained thing to do! "OK, Mare. What do you want?"

"Oh, I gotta think about this!" she gloated. "This can't be rushed. Give me a minute."

Our food came, and we began eating. Right in the middle of a forkful of spaghetti, Marilyn said, "I've got it. Oh. This is *great*. I've *got* it!" I was hoping she meant ptomaine poisoning, but she continued, "I won the bet fair and square, so you have to promise me you'll do it. 'No matter what,' we said, so you have to do this. Agreed?"

"Yes, Marilyn, I'll do it. Of course. Whatever you ask, I'll do it. Just tell me." Little did I know I was about to be embarrassed out of my mind.

"When we get ready to leave tonight, you go up to this woman we think is Mrs. Banducci, introduce yourself by name, and say to her very seriously, 'Mrs. Banducci, my Chihuahua is so much better. Thank you for your prayers.' That's it. You can't tell her it's a bet. Just say that and walk away like you've got good sense."

She was hysterical with laughter.

"You want me to WHAT? You're crazy, Marilyn! Nothing in the world could make me do that. That woman will think I'm nuts."

"I know it. She sure will. That's the whole point!" she said, between shrieks. "But you promised—remember? You said, 'No matter what!'"

I was so sick at my stomach I could hardly finish my meal. I tried practicing my line; I prayed the floor would open and suck me under it. I wanted to run away. Every escape route went through my mind. And the nearer the time came for our departure, the sicker I got. I was a pitiful sight as Marilyn chowed down and kept laughing.

I dragged out the meal as long as I could. My stomach was in knots. I asked Marilyn if she'd wait for me outside. Smiling, she pronounced, "Wild horses could not wrench me from your side, my dear." My hour of death had come!

Mrs. Banducci was standing at the cash register when we walked up. Her back was to me, so I cleared my throat. She turned around and flashed a big smile.

"Are you Mrs. Banducci?" I asked.

"Well, yes, I am," she replied, still smiling.

God help you, woman! I wanted to scream, but instead I reminded myself, *If you're going to do this, Luci, do it good. Be very serious, and do your best job.* I continued, "It's so nice to meet you, Mrs. Banducci. My name is Luci Swindoll, and my friend and I are here from Fullerton for a visit." I glanced stern-faced to Marilyn, who was leaning in the doorway with her arms crossed. "Before we leave tonight, I just wanted you to know my Chihuahua is so much better. Thank you for your prayers."

I stood tall, didn't smile, and looked the woman straight in the face, implacable and unmoved by my duty. I'm not quite sure what I felt at that moment, but I hope to never feel it again. It was a cross between agony and the desire to kill. And poor Mrs. Banducci? Well, the smile she had had on her face all evening now turned to a quizzical frown; she put both hands on my shoulders and said kindly, "Honey, you and your friend come back."

"Oh, we will, Mrs. Banducci. We *certainly* will," I lied. I paid the check and walked outside to find Marilyn reeling down the sidewalk, hardly able to catch her breath she was laughing so uncontrollably. We both laughed for hours. Even during the night when one of us awakened, our hoots of laughter awoke the other. It was truly the most comical, idiotic, embarrassing thing I've ever done. And to think, I did it *on purpose*.

The next morning as we were driving away from Palm Springs, we passed that restaurant and Marilyn had the gall to say, "I'll give you fifty bucks if you go in there and tell that woman your Chihuahua died."

Laugh with Others

"I don't need the money, thank you!"

To this day, we laugh over that story. And believe it or not . . . we keep making bets! Today, we live only a couple of blocks apart in Frisco, Texas, and the bets are still on. I won one a few weeks ago over something that happened in Marilyn's driveway. Always lots of fun!

Learn to Laugh at Life

More often than not, though, life is serious. There's a lot of heartache and sorrow in it. But listen to me—if you can laugh at it, you can live with it!

Very few people are as comical and off the wall as Marilyn, and we can't expect them to be. We get in trouble when we require a person to step out of her temperament and become a comedian just to keep us happy. It would be my preference for everybody in the world to have a sense of humor, but this is simply not the way God has designed us.

I can't tell you the number of times women come to my table at a Women of Faith conference and tell me it's been months (or sometimes years) since they laughed. They'll even say, "We never laughed when I was growing up, and I never learned how. My parents had no time for that. How can I learn to laugh?" Oh my! That's a tough one.

When people ask me that question, I tell them not to

take themselves so seriously. They can't redo the past, but they can start looking for comedy in the nooks and crannies of life here and now. Yes, life is hard, but that doesn't mean that people have to be hard too. I encourage others to try to find funny things in everyday circumstances and to give themselves permission to laugh at those things.

But I *never* tell them to work on changing their temperaments. If you have a melancholy temperament, try your best to stay away from negative people. Negativism pulls us down. It makes us cranky, and we pick up the offenses of the negative person. Sure, things are wrong all around us, but don't sit in that pot and stew. Make up your mind that you're not going to keep living a negative life. Lighten up. Forgive your own mistakes.

Also, know this—don't waste time trying to change somebody. If you'd like a person to be different, there are two positive things you can do. First, you can pray for that person—and keep at it when the chips are down. Pray without stopping, and believe the answer will come. Second, model how you'd like that person to be if you *could* change him or her. If you'd like that person to be more loving, you love. More understanding, you be that way. If you'd like your friend to be punctual, then you must be punctual. Modeling is a better beginning than confronting.

I used to sing with the Dallas Opera Company (in the late 1950s through the early '70s), and I had a friend who hardly ever laughed. She was sweet and had one of the most gorgeous voices I've ever heard, but when it came to the personality department, she was like talking to a stick. No warmth. Nothing about her caused me to want to pursue her friendship. But she liked me. During our rehearsal time, she often asked me to join her at breaks to visit a bit. That was hard for me because I preferred being with my laughing, fun, closer friends, but I didn't want to hurt her feelings by telling her no. I felt a sort of "holy nudge," you might say, so I said sure. She requested little, but even that seems hard when people don't give much themselves.

At the time I was very involved in a wonderful Bible church where God's truth was being taught. Somehow, she'd heard that I went to church. During our visits, she began asking questions about my faith, and as I answered and opened my heart, she opened up too. She confessed having been severely abused as a child. Coming from a home where her parents were mean and exceedingly strict had so squelched her spirit that she was afraid to laugh. Everything in her parents' home was built on discipline, obedience, and faultfinding. Now she was grown, but she seemed unable to escape the overhanging shadow of that rigid background.

One evening during our chat, I invited her to go with me to church the following Sunday, and she accepted. As she stood by me in the worship service, her gorgeous voice filled the sanctuary. Her heart was in it and I could feel it, as could those around me.

As those weeks passed, she continued to attend church with me, where she was asked to sing a few solos. In time, she went with me to Bible class and received Christ as Savior. I watched this woman literally change before my eyes. She thoroughly enjoyed being a part of that church, and her spiritual growth was phenomenal. Her temperament didn't change . . . but her heart did. She began to laugh and have a bit of fun. She didn't become a comic, but her soul was softened by laughter.

If you're looking for companionship that's laced with humor, let yourself go a little bit and when you feel like being funny or doing a comedy act for your friend, do it. Don't wait for her to go first. Model what you want . . . all the while remembering we can't require people to have a different temperament than what they have. Let them be themselves and you be yourself, then watch what God does.

11 Laugh with Yourself

When I got up this morning, I was expecting a couple of pieces of patio furniture to be delivered, so I dressed up. Well, for me it was dressing up. I wore "a little outfit." Black. Always my color of choice. I'm not much for little outfits, but my friend Mary swears by them. And she *always* looks like a million bucks. Every now and then, she'll say something to me like, "You're having your picture made today for your driver's license, Luci. You might want to wear a little outfit." Or, "You looked so nice yesterday on the plane in your little outfit." Or, "Would you like for me to look at a little outfit for you today when I run down to the mall?"

Left up to me, I'd never (maybe "rarely" is more accurate) wear a little outfit, because I don't really care if things match. They can be faded, old, ill fitting, and ripped . . . but if they're comfortable, I'll wear 'em.

Enough about that.

Knowing the furniture men were coming this morning and that I needed to run an errand immediately thereafter, I put on a little outfit and looked fairly presentable, if I do say so myself. Everything matched. Mary would have been proud.

So I'm standing at the kitchen counter in my little outfit, eating a piece of toast smeared with wild plum jelly, enjoying the moment, and thinking about my work for the day when something very unexpected happened. I turned my hand the wrong way, and before I could stop it, the toast with smeared jelly had fallen on my shirt right square in the front, covering a space of about three by six inches. *Oh no! My little outfit!*

I just stood there for a moment. Finally looking down, I saw plum jelly everywhere. I laughed heartily. "What a way to start a day," I said to the sink. "This is exactly what I'm talking about in this book."

I've had so many occasions like this when I could have cried over a circumstance like that jelly thing and chose not to . . . times when humor was born out of a predicament . . . times when I consciously set about to create a few rays of light on a dark horizon.

Case in point: I was invited to sing at my nephew's wedding a number of years ago, which was held in a large church and officiated by the two fathers (of both bride and groom), who were both ministers. Months of work had gone into this event, and I'd been advised of the colors and told, "It might be a good idea to wear a little outfit to match." Gotcha! I can do that!

It so happened I had a formal in those exact colors, so rather than buy something new and spend money I didn't have, I decided to wear the dress in my closet. Admittedly, this dress had been around awhile, but it would certainly do for one evening. After all, I was just the soloist, not the bride, thank you very much.

I dashed off to the cleaners to ask their advice on letting out the hem, patching a small hole at the neckline, and having it cleaned and pressed. They assured me they would be able to do it all and in plenty of time for the big event. I left there very pleased, feeling rather smug and jubilant about the whole thing.

On the morning of the wedding I picked up the dress, and it did indeed look terrific. I brought it home and, about two hours before I was due at the church, decided to try it on just to be sure everything was all I had hoped. Great. It was perfect! I sat down to put on a pair of heels I had planned to wear with it, but just as I stood to look in the mirror one last time, my right heel caught in the hem, and I heard, *Rrrrrrriip!* Without looking, I sat down again and put my head in my hands. I counted to ten. I took a deep breath. Then I counted to ten again. To God, I whispered, "This cannot be. It just *cannot*. What am I going to do, Lord? I can't look down . . . but did You hear that rip? I've probably torn the back out of this old thing. What now?"

I was afraid to look at the damage, when suddenly it struck me: *Luci, this isn't the end of the world. This is an inconvenience, not a catastrophe. Life is going to go on whether you sing or not. Whether this wedding goes on or not. Now shape up, kid. Think of something; be creative. Use your imagination.* And I began to laugh. I don't really know why, but I did. It was like this morning's plum jelly incident. The incongruity of the turn of events in light of my preparations struck me as funny, and all I could do was laugh.

I finally got up, and sure enough, there was a large, irregular tear just above the hemline. I dashed back to the cleaners to see if they could repair it hurriedly. They did while I waited. Then I told myself, "I'll wear this old rag as its swan song before it retires from active duty, and for everybody who says anything positive about the dress, I'll take five dollars out of my savings account and put it in a fund toward a new dress."

I added two requirements: (1) The comment had to have the word "dress" in it, not just "You really look nice tonight" or some such nonsense, and (2) I could not tell anyone about this until it was over. It was a private contest between my ego and my little outfit.

For the first time, I got excited about the wedding.

During the course of the evening, I received six direct compliments about that formal. Can you believe it? One dear old man said, "Luci, you look so pretty. Is that a new dress?" Of course, he was nearly blind, but I counted it for five bucks just the same. I loved that whole occasion, and my old dress made thirty dollars before the evening was over. Bingo!

As I was getting ready for bed that night, I was glad I had reacted to that problem with a laugh. I thought about it for a long time . . . not the dress or the occasion so much as why it's important to respond with a sense of humor when things don't go our way. So often we pick a fight with ourselves, get our feelings hurt, or look for somebody to blame. But if we stay that way, we'll never escape our own predicament.

Have Fun in the Moment

I advocate having a little fun while you're in the moment. *You* make it into fun instead of failure. No one can do it for you. We're responsible for ourselves. In this instance, I could have gone out and bought a new dress, but why do that? My budget wouldn't permit it, and my good sense told me to be creative. A creative contest with an opportunity to laugh and have fun. My kind of thing!

How do you react to life's unpleasant circumstances? Do you look for ways to find happiness and joy or do you just give in . . . give up, and join the ranks of the "if-any-thing-bad-can-happen-it-will-happen-to-me" people? Granted, every dilemma doesn't have a humorous side, but I believe more do than we realize.

Here are a few principles that have helped me thrive through disappointments, turning around a difficult circumstance. Remember these when the chips are down:

- Realize most problems are inconveniences, not catastrophes.
- Don't take yourself too seriously, and stop being so literal.
- Count your blessings instead of your blunders.
- Take everything as a compliment.
- Enjoy your freedom because Christ has set you free.

- Look for the funny side of everything even if it's teensy-weensy.
- Don't sweat the small stuff.
- Do something fun just for yourself that makes you laugh.

Have Fun Just for You

That last principle reminds me of the time I came home from work—tired, lonely, and fed up with life. I was in a bad mood after driving an hour on a crowded freeway. All I wanted to do was get out of my office clothes and relax with no interruptions. I kept thinking, *If I could have a good laugh, that would help.* This was before the days of the Internet, but I knew if I could just connect with somebody I loved, I'd feel better. I went to the mailbox to find solace, but the only piece of mail I got was a postcard delivered to my house by mistake. *Even the mail is against me,* I thought.

I decided to read the postcard and see if there was anything in it to cheer me up. But it was the most inane communiqué I'd ever seen. It read:

Dear Jane,

The drive here was nice. We stopped for a bite to eat at a nice place on the way. The coffee was cold but the food was pretty good. Stanley said their gravy tasted as good as mine but I think mine's better. We sure are having a nice time. See you soon.

Bye-bye and love,

Dorothy

Poor Jane. She deserved something better than that. "That's an awful message," I said to myself. "Maybe I'll help Dorothy with this note. Let's see . . . what can I add that will help? I think I'll jot a line at the bottom." I practiced scribbling out my thoughts on a piece of scratch paper to achieve the same style of writing, using the same size pen point and color. Then I added: "P.S. Jerry's leg is so much better. Practically healed," and dropped it in the mailbox.

Don't you think that helped? It would not only give the reader something to ponder, but as I dropped it in the box, it gave me the laugh I was looking for. Was that cruel? Do you think it caused someone to worry unnecessarily? I've heard that the coarsest type of humor is the practical joke, but this had no malicious intent. It was a crazy gag, done in fun . . . just for me, to make me laugh. And it worked,

Fortunately, this nutty strain runs in my family. My two brothers and I have actually fallen over laughing at life's incongruities. Chuck preached our mother's funeral back in February 1971, and when we all got to his house afterward, he was changing from his black suit into sweats. Noticing something small under his white dress shirt, we asked him if it was a bandage. Had he cut himself or something? He said he had felt a lump under his right arm while he was preaching. When he took off his shirt, he realized it was his youngest son's baby sock. Chuck had "worn" it during the entire funeral service. It had stuck to the shirt when it came out of the dryer. We all howled, even in the midst of our grieving for mother and talked about how much she would have loved that moment as much as we.

Please don't take yourself too seriously. Life will be a lot more fun if you learn to lighten up and laugh!

12 Laugh with God

At a recent Women of Faith conference, I had an interesting discussion with an attendee. She was bright, articulate, and soft-spoken. Sharp eyes and an engaging smile. She came to my book table to have one of our devotional books signed on Friday night before anything really got rolling.

As I was inscribing the book, I asked, "How are you? Is this your first time at Women of Faith?"

"Yes, it is," she responded rather timidly. "I've wanted to come for a long time, but my father's ill, so it's hard to get away."

"I understand. Caring for a sick parent can be very tiring and emotionally draining. My father was sick for a long time, too, and sometimes it was hard for me to leave him. But I'm so glad you're here, and I hope you have a great time." I thought that was the end of our conversation, because she kind of turned to walk away with her book. Then she looked back over her shoulder and asked, "Does God ever laugh?"

I thought about it and then said, "Yes. The Bible talks about God laughing from to time. Why do you ask?"

She turned around and came back. "The other day my dad and I were talking, and he said, 'You know, one reason I look forward to heaven is so God and I can have a big laugh together. That'll really make me happy.' My dad's had a very hard life, and it thrills me to think he and God will laugh together someday. Then I got to wondering, *Does God laugh?* I figured you'd know, being a Christian speaker and all."

Then I laughed.

The Laughter of God

Laughter's a tough subject when it comes to God. We often read in the Bible about His attributes of love, mercy, goodness, grace, forgiveness, even joy . . . but laughter? Not much. When God laughs, it signifies something he despises or mocks. Take Psalm 2 for example. David is writing about the nations of the earth conspiring or plotting against the Lord. He's questioning their effrontery as they volley for international position or meet for summit talks. (David thinks it was bad in *his* day . . . he should live in the twenty-first century). Then, in verse 4, he describes how God feels about that: "The One enthroned in heaven laughs; the Lord scoffs at them" (NIV). Or, as Eugene Petersen puts it in *The Message*, "Heaven-throned God breaks out laughing." He is furious at this kind of behavior.

Psalm 59 has an interesting group of verses where David pleads with God to protect him from his enemies—those who have come to kill him. In verse 8, he says, "Lord, laugh at them! (And scoff at these surrounding nations too)" (TLB). And finally, in Psalm 37:12–13, David is very straightforward: "The wicked plot against the righteous and gnash their teeth at them; but the Lord laughs at the wicked, for he knows their day is coming" (NIV). Nothing could be clearer than that. The Lord can easily laugh at these situations because He knows the outcome. God's laughter is not to be disregarded or questioned.

The Laughter of God's Children

But having said that, God's laughter at the folly of mankind is not the laughter to which I refer in this chapter. Laughing *with* God is another thing entirely. When we know God personally through the work of His Son, Jesus Christ, on the cross and we have invited Him into our heart as our Savior, we learn we can laugh in God's presence and He laughs with us. It may not be recorded in Scripture with clear definition, but I know full well that God has created us to be happy and full of joy. Nehemiah 8:10 says, "The joy of the LORD is your strength." And part of that joy is laughter.

When I think of laughing with God, I refer to those ways He communicates with us where we're comfortable settling into His presence. When we do things to please Him, bring honor to Him, share His grace with others, and exercise the gifts he's given us, I picture God laughing. I believe when we reflect who He is, He laughs. He's happy.

Here's an illustration of what I mean: when I was growing up, my family talked a lot about the Bible—going in, coming out, sitting around—the Bible was a common topic in our house. We were a verbal bunch anyway, but one of our favorite topics was God's Word. We memorized scriptures, asked each other what we thought different verses meant, and kept little books and/or cards with different scriptures on them that we were trying to learn by heart and use in our lives. This was very important to my parents and, in time, to their three kids as well. My brothers and I are the richer for it today.

It was during this time that I remember discovering Job 23:10–11: "But he knows every detail of what is happening to me; and when he has examined me, he will pronounce me completely innocent—as pure as solid gold! I have stayed in God's paths, following his steps. I have not turned aside. I have not refused his commandments but have enjoyed them more than my daily food" (TLB).

Stop there a minute. See that last part that reads, "I . . . have enjoyed them more than my daily food"? That's very important, because the principle is that when God's children (anyone who has put their faith in His Son) make the Bible a topic of conversation, we are being fed in a way that's more important than eating our daily food from the table. If we go a step further and memorize scriptures, seal those words in our heart, and use them when trouble comes . . . that spiritual food pays off in even richer ways, personally. It enables us to fight the enemy just like a good diet helps us battle enemies to our physical bodies.

Now, I look at my life and those of my brothers—all of us in public Christian ministry—and I cannot help but wonder if by continually eating spiritual food as we were growing up that we became stronger in ministry as adults. Does this not please God? When we learn of Him and talk about what He likes and who He is and why He cares, are we not bringing Him joy? Is it not conceivable that He is laughing in delight? Many has been the time when all of us (and I do this now with my friends) were tickled . . . laughing out loud . . . at some 'find' we had made about God's Word because we were so elated over the discovery. A scripture that we found pleased us so much or suddenly made sense or thrilled our socks off . . . and we laughed.

When Chuck was a student at Dallas Theological Seminary, on more than one occasion he called me to share some new thing he had learned about Scripture or God in one of the original languages in which the Bible was written, and he was laughing his head off out of sheer joy. This is the best way to learn anything—to be thrilled about seeing it and having it sink in!

That is laughing with God.

The Laughter of Giving

What about giving? Not just tithing, but giving beyond your tithe—having a generous heart where God is honored because of human generosity. Look at Psalm 112. The whole chapter is about what happens to the person who has a generous spirit toward others. The opening verse starts the ball rolling with praise. "Praise the LORD!" it says.

If you fear God and trust Him, you're blessed beyond expression. You're happy. You laugh. Your good deeds are never forgotten and they never stop because you're always thinking of ways to give away what you have.

The joy of making money will be realized in giving it away. Look particularly at Psalm 112:9: "He gives generously to those in need. His deeds will never be forgotten. He shall have influence and honor" (TLB). Do you see the pattern here? A generous heart makes God happy. Maybe it makes Him laugh. It certainly makes me laugh when I'm able to help others by giving them something. If it means the world to me, how do you think it makes God feel?

This is laughing with God.

The Laughter of Getting Along

And here's one more example: Proverbs 16:7 says, "When a man's ways are pleasing to the LORD, he makes even his enemies live at peace with him" (NIV). Look at that. No vengeance. No retribution. No getting even. Just please the Lord, and your enemies become peaceful.

The most vivid use of this scripture that I've ever heard was by Jim Voss, a member of the Mickey Cohen tough-guy squad when he came to know Christ as his personal Savior. He gave his testimony one night at a church I was attending. Jim had been deeply involved in crime. But by the time I heard him, he was a strong advocate of grace. As you can imagine, that did not go well with the mob. They were ready to kill him because of his newfound faith.

Jim decided early on that he would not betray any of the members of the Cohen mob, but at the same time, he would clean up his own act and see where God took him. One of the first things he decided to do was to make a list of all the people he had robbed, cheated, lied to, hated, and worse . . . and then go through the list and make things right with every individual—whatever that meant and for however long it took. After trying to recall each name and writing it down, his list filled nine single-spaced, typed pages, naming hundreds of persons whom he needed to contact. And he kept his word.

During this period of his life, Jim and his wife were at their home one night when several members of the Mickey Cohen mob came to his front door, armed with guns and ready for trouble. That night, Jim Voss claimed this verse—Proverbs 16:7—and went to the door with fear and trembling but determined that no matter what he would honor the Lord with his words. When he was harassed and accused and badgered by these men, he stood his ground and kindly told them the truth about what had happened to him and his plans to pay back those he had wronged. He implicated no one else. He simply believed that what he was doing was the right thing and that God delivered him from the mob. "After about ten minutes," he said, "they left, and I went back inside and sat down and thanked God." Even his enemies were at peace with him.

That is laughing with God.

Although not necessarily funny or amusing, this kind of laughter is rooted in profound truth that produces unspeakable joy. It gives happy satisfaction to the heart of the believer who knows how pleased it makes God when we apply the truth of His Word.

During the lifetime of Christ and the apostle Paul, there lived a man named Philo of Alexandria. (The first-century historian Josephus talks about him in his book *Antiquities of the Jews*.) In one of Philo's essays, called "The Worse Attacks the Better," he says this wonderful line: "God is the creator of laughter that is good." And that's the kind of laughter I'm talking about.

"Laughter that is good" is an interesting phrase, because there is much laughter that is not good—not character building or helpful to those around us. It is never acceptable to laugh at someone else's expense, though people do it a lot. I would encourage you to guard against that. Our friends and acquaintances can be decimated by ill-placed or poorly timed humor. Looking back over my life, I recall times when I made comments that were inopportune or out of place, and I wish so much that I could retract those statements. If I had that to do over again, I would say things so differently . . . or better still, say nothing at all. I've rarely regretted something I didn't say but have often regretted what I did say. I'm older and wiser now, but I realize that's an important truth to learn and one I want to pass along to you.

The Last Laugh

Not only have I been asked if God laughs, but I'm sometimes asked, "Is God funny?" or, "Is there anything about Him that's funny?" Yes, there are a lot of things that make me think God has a sense of humor. Maybe it's my quirky sense of humor, but when I think of some of the animals He's made, I know He laughs. Or situations that are so weird, nobody could put all the parts together but God. Even answers to prayer are hilarious sometimes. I think He laughs often.

Personally, I think the last laugh on earth will come from God. It will sound "like the laughter of the universe," as Dante said in his allegory *The Divine Comedy*. When the Easter story is completed, the risen Christ will come to earth again and take us with Him to heaven. Scripture says, "We'll be walking on air!" (1 Thessalonians 4:18 MSG).

And God Himself will have the last laugh. The entire universe will be proclaiming the love of God in Christ Jesus—and then we'll all laugh together, celebrating our risen and reigning Lord.

part four

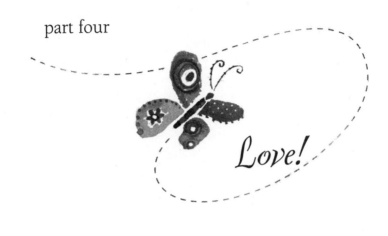

Love!

13 Love What You're Doing

I walked into the Public Works office in Culver City, California, one afternoon to get a building permit when I worked for Mobil Oil, and I saw a small sign posted on a bulletin board to my right. It read: "If you don't believe in the resurrection of the dead, stick around here until 5:00."

I was tempted to take down that sign, put it in my billfold, go by Kinko's on the way home, and make twenty copies to post in every workplace I frequented. That observation applied to people at my beauty shop, supermarket, service station, department store, and church. I can't tell you the hundreds of times I've seen people drag through work because they hated it so much or listened to them gripe endlessly about their job. They literally live for the closing bell to sound on their shift.

In fact, I was shopping for a Thanksgiving dinner several years ago, and while I was waiting for my groceries to be added up and bagged, two checkers were talking over the heads of people about when they could go home. I remember it well because I wrote it down when I got in the car so I would never forget it:

"When did you clock in?"

"At ten. Did you?"

"Yeah."

"I didn't want to come to work today."

"Me neither."

"I hate this job."

"Me too. I can't wait to get off. Gotta study for a test."

"Oh yeah? In what?"

"Finance."

"That's your major, right?"

"No, my major's business."

Everybody waiting in line rolled their eyes at one another, and I personally wanted to scream, "Get a job you like or just shut up!" But the truth is, there is no job those kids like. They've grown up griping because their parents griped and they let their kids gripe, so why not go to their graves griping? Everybody does it. And to think, one of them was majoring in business. Someday, he's going to be your daughter's boss, and he's going to hate his job then too. Or, hopefully the tables will turn, and your daughter will be his boss . . . if he passes his finance test.

Being content in a job is one of the hardest things in the world unless you're absolutely called to that profession or have learned it's possible to be content anywhere. Many jobs serve as a means unto an end, and we'd like that end to be right now. They are what my friend Thelma Wells calls "the meantime," and the meanness of that time often drags us so far down that we want to give up and walk away. We hate the job, we hate the other employees, but mostly we hate ourselves. I've been there, you've been there, and we both know people who are there now. It's part of the human condition. There's a battle going on between hating and waiting. We hate where we are, but we're waiting for something to get better.

Here's what I'm realizing as I get older and older—the battle that rages is not in the job at all. It's in us. It actually has nothing to do with the job or the workplace itself. It has to do with being human. We don't like where we are because we can't find peace within ourselves. And we will always go through life feeling that way until we come to terms with the fact that every difficult thing starts within our own heart. It's about attitude.

Larry Crabb has written an insightful book on this very issue, called *Inside Out*.[1] In this book, he says the ache that we feel inside—waiting and hoping for situations to get better—is not neurosis or spiritual immaturity; it's reality. But there's more: because we can't do anything to escape that ache, most of us either keep griping or deny it exists and live in some sort of la-la land pretending everything's hunky-dory. Neither of these scenarios works.

So what can we do? Is there any way for us to find joy in our environment—any way to love what we're doing?

Yes, there most definitely is. Here are the steps I'm learning to take. When I stick with these over the long haul, I find I don't complain, I don't wait for something to get better before I get joyful, and I have more patience with myself and others. I'm not saying it's easy . . . but I do believe it's possible.

Face the Fact That Life on Earth Is Profoundly Disappointing

This goes back to what I was saying in chapter 9 when I talked about shifting the weight of this fact onto God. There will be tests, there will be challenges, and there will be tough times. You can't change that fact. That's a non-negotiable part of living. Face it, and don't forget it.

I've often said if someone had just told me when I was young to lower my expectations about life, it would have been easier along the way. But now, I'm not sure my elders knew that for themselves. I always expected so much. And granted, I've had some wonderful times in my life, but within my heart somewhere there was always a feeling of being incomplete. It's what I used to call a "cosmic sadness." I couldn't put my finger on it, but I felt it. So if you feel that, too, welcome to the human race. You're right on target.

Learn to Love the Struggle

What most of us do (like those two guys at the grocery store checkout) is bemoan our fate. We want to get off work. We want to go home. We want to get rid of the rules. We want more freedom. We want anything but *this*. Because *this* is the thing we feel that pulls our spirit down and/or confines us. It's that cosmic sadness. You'll take it with you wherever you go, for as long as you live. So you have to learn to love that part of life.

How do we do that? I'm glad you asked. We look at things inside ourselves that need changing. Things like painful memories, destructive patterns and emotions, hidden agendas, hurtful relationships, mistakes we've made but haven't forgiven, our parents' mistakes, histrionic behavior. The list is longer than this, but you get the picture. Until we start admitting these things need work to change, there's no way we can reach spiritual maturity or love the struggle that is part of being alive. And we can't love where we are until we address who we are inside, warts and all. This is the struggle we all face, and we have to see it, accept it, and love it . . . no matter what.

But how can we love what we don't like about ourselves? Go to the next step.

Instead of Protecting Yourself, Pursue God

It's our human nature to protect ourselves from pain. Rare is the person who purposely walks into something that hurts. Most of us want to run in the other direction. We throw up all sorts of barriers to keep out the "slings and arrows" of outrageous anxiety. It's the defense we use because we don't want to feel bad. That makes perfect sense to us humans. But this isn't God's way. God says, "Come to Me if you're weak or if you've got burdens or pain. Put your problems on Me, and I will give you rest" (see Matthew 11:28). God cares about us and wants us to trust Him with these things that drive us crazy. So instead of protecting ourselves, His invitation is for us to pursue Him and to accept what He offers to give us, which is enduring peace and joy, even in the midst of life's disappointments.

When we deny our pain or pretend we're comfortable on the inside, we're not pursuing God. We're depending on our own strength to cope with a cosmic sadness that's impossible for us to fix without help from One who is stronger than we.

And here's a little interesting sideline blessing: the people who spend the most time pursuing God might feel the most disappointment, because they know how things should be, making reality all the more ugly and unbearable. And this is good, you ask? Yes! It's good. In the words of Larry Crabb, "Honest people touch the inevitable distress of life."[2] But the beauty of this honesty is being aware of the reason you feel what you feel—knowing the difference, knowing the why of the sadness, thus giving credence for loving where you are in life! And this my friends, is why we can celebrate life even when we know it is profoundly disappointing: because we know the difference, and we know the why of that difference.

Conduct Your Own Investigation About Tough Issues

Admit nothing is perfect, and keep going. Keep loving. Keep pursuing God. Eventually, there will be obvious growth. You will feel it inside, and you'll recognize that you've come a long way. Try your best not to be bound in the shackles of legalism. Instead, investigate what Christ says about being set free to live, and thrive in the liberty He offers. Look at everything in your life, no matter how confused that might make you. In the long run, you'll be untangling the threads that lead to that which has tied you in knots for years. It won't be easy, but it will be worth it.

All this to say, "Love what you're doing"? Yes, I believe this is what it takes. At least, it's what it has taken for me to grow up. If we keep going through life letting the battles and the struggles pull us down, no matter what we do, we won't be content anywhere. We'll always be looking for something better, somewhere else. We'll want to live somewhere else, be married to somebody else, or have another job. But contentment doesn't lie in doing something else. It lies inside us, waiting to be tapped. And this is how to tap it—get acquainted with God as intimately as possible. Job 22:21 says, "Now acquaint yourself with Him, and be at peace; thereby good will come to you" (NKJV).

In 1974, I pulled up stakes in my home state of Texas and moved to California to try something different. I was young and idealistic, and I thought California would be heaven on earth. Why? I don't know. Maybe because I hadn't lived anywhere but Texas, and my idea of California held a lot of what I look for in life—adventure, challenge, and new vistas. I was up for it. I transferred from one branch of Mobil Oil Corporation to another, packed up and moved. I threw myself into a new state, new job, new church, and new home. Even new friends. But as time went on, I realized I wasn't happy . . . with anything. Nothing lived up to my expectations. Something was wrong with everything. And it didn't get better.

As the months passed, I wondered if I had done the wrong thing. I fretted. I pouted. I ranted. I cried. All I could think of was getting off work every day and going home and staying there . . . and dying there. I hated my job, I hated the state, and most of all, I hated myself. The disappointment was profound. I spent all my time trying to figure out what was wrong with me and hating myself for moving away from Texas. There was nothing about my situation I could control. It was out of my hands. I felt stuck. And I *really* hated that!

After two years had passed, one afternoon on my hour's drive home, I was crying and carrying on with my usual diatribe when God suddenly broke through the mental chatter and said, *Why don't you quit griping, let go, shut up, and just trust Me? I'm in charge of your life, Luci. Not you. Got that? You'll never be happy until you quit fighting Me.* He went on . . . a monologue I heard in my head, as though my father had set me down to make a very serious point. I was listening. Finally!

I got home that day and felt a bit different. I felt better somehow, even after being chastened by God's Spirit. Not a single thing in my life had changed, but I felt that maybe I had changed, or was beginning to. I made up my mind that day that no matter what, I was going to take my hands off trying to control everything. I decided even if God took my life, I was going to quit fighting for everything to be my way. The old had passed away; God was trying to do something new, and I was standing in the way of it. So I let go for the first time.

In the days ahead, I started pursuing Him. I began to read everything I could in Scripture about tribulation, tests, burdens, and disappointments . . . and I put myself in those biblical situations. In each case, the Bible says to trust God; let Him do what He wants to, and things will work out. I prayed about my work situation. I even began to believe things might get better for me, although I no longer waited nor longed for that to happen. I just kept doing the next thing . . . but with a different motive.

Not long after I heard God's monologue during my road rage, I was offered another job within Mobil, and I took it. During the four years I held that job, I saw over and over how I could have never performed the duties required had I not learned certain skills from my previous job, which I had so hated. God had used that frustrating job to prepare me for the enjoyable one He had planned for me. And the next job was to a management position with Mobil; I was the first woman to become a manager in that branch of Mobil on the West Coast. During my tenure as a manager, I turned fifty-five and took early retirement in order to spend the rest of my life speaking and writing. I had worked thirty years with Mobil when I retired, and God had used it as my battleground. It was there He proved himself to be my faithful, worthy, consistent overseer.

I never in my life wanted or planned to climb the corporate ladder at Mobil. I've often been asked how I got from being a draftsman to becoming a manager. What was my strategy for getting ahead? I can honestly say I had none. I simply kept on keeping on. I didn't quit when I wanted to. I didn't sink when I was barely treading water. God kept me afloat, and I kept paddling.

I don't believe we can plan those kinds of promotions for ourselves, frankly. If we do the very best we can and stay intimately acquainted with God, I believe He'll open and close the doors that He chooses for us. It won't be up to us. It's really true that if we're faithful in the little things, He turns over bigger and bigger things for us to handle. By the time certain God-ordained opportunities come along, we will have learned some of life's most important lessons that will help us do the job at hand. And we will love where we are!

God knew what he was doing in my work life all along. When the door closed to secular work, He opened one to Christian work. And He hasn't stopped yet. Every day, I have to renew my energies and desires in Him. Even writing this book is an enormous undertaking and commitment, and I don't know if I will finish my manuscript on time. But all I can do is the next thing, every day. That's all any of us can do. We think, pray, study, learn, and start out. And where God takes us next is up to Him.

I like that now. It took me a long time to get here, but when I experience the good that has come to me, I'm so glad I made peace with Him.

14 Love Though It's Painful

While I was working in the petroleum industry, I had occasion to meet with a man who owned a commercial nursery. He managed large accounts that furnished plants, trees, flowers, and shrubs for commercial buildings and open-air locations. His business was thriving. At Mobil Oil Corporation, where I worked, we were attempting to acquire an easement across his property to lay a pipeline that would transfer oil from point A to point B. In connection with that, I negotiated with him over a period of time; and after a few months of discussion, the deed was drawn up and signed by all parties to our mutual satisfaction. I found him to be a very amenable person to work with, and we always had cheerful conversations. (Let's call this guy Abel Miller, since I'm not at liberty to give you his real name.)

During that same year, I often went to a little flower shop not too far from Mr. Miller's business to order bouquets for various events at my office. One day while I was waiting for the salesperson to write up my receipt, I met the owner of the shop. He was charming, verbal, and artistic with flowers. I ultimately came to realize he knew plants and their habitats like the back of his hand. After telling him who I was and why I shopped there so often, he graciously introduced himself as Cain Miller.

"Oh my," I said laughingly. "You don't happen to be the brother of Abel Miller, do you . . . that guy who owns the big nursery?" I thought it might be a long shot, but since the two men had the same last name and were in similar businesses, there might be a connection.

Without very much emotion, he said, "Yes. He's my brother."

"He's the nicest guy," I said. "I've done business with him in the last few months to lay a pipeline across his property."

"That's *my* property," Cain insisted.

"Oh, I didn't know that. The deed is in his name. Do you own it together?" I was a little confused at this point.

Although I didn't want to probe, I was hoping for more information.

He wasn't reluctant to give it, even though we had never had more than a casual chat. "No. He owns it, but by all rights, it's mine."

"What do you mean?" Cain didn't seem the least embarrassed to open up about his family's private business, although I was virtually a complete stranger. Maybe he thought I looked like a psychologist. By now his tone was very serious, and he seemed eager to get the story on the table.

"Well," he said, "my dad and I own this little shop, and my mother and brother own that big piece of land. My grandparents willed it to all of us when they died, but somehow Dad and I wound up with this small part, and Mom and Abel got the other part. I'm in the process of suing them now."

"You're suing your mother and brother?" I asked, not knowing families did that to each other.

"Yeah. I'm taking them to court. Dad and I want to show them they can't do this and get away with it."

"Well, that's terrible," I said. "I hate that for your family; it's a horrible breach. Have you ever thought of sitting down and having a family meeting, to talk it through?"

"Oh yeah . . . but they don't want to. They treat us like

dirt, and we always wind up with the short end of the stick. So I'm suing them."

"How long has this been going on?" I asked in my naiveté and genuinely eager to know.

"Three years. We've not spoken to them in three years."

I was stunned! *Three years.* "Wow, that's a long time. What would happen if all of you sat down, negotiated on a level playing field, and everybody tried to understand and forgive each other?"

Then Cain said the most interesting thing: "Forgive? I'll never do that. Forgiveness is a myth, and it never works . . . I'd rather carry a grudge than to forgive. I want what's rightfully mine, and I'm gonna get it."

Cain and Abel. Two brothers who couldn't get along, wouldn't forgive, and wound up archenemies. Cain thought forgiveness was a myth and that it never worked. With that attitude, there was no hope for reconciliation.

Love Through the Pain

As long as we carry a grudge and want to get even, it's impossible to love. The last three verses of Ephesians 4 make that very clear: "Don't grieve God. Don't break his heart. His Holy Spirit, moving and breathing in you, is the most intimate part of your life, making you fit for himself.

Don't take such a gift for granted. Make a clean break with all cutting, backbiting, profane talk. Be gentle with one another, sensitive. Forgive one another as quickly and thoroughly as God in Christ forgave you" (vv. 30–32 MSG).

I don't believe unforgiveness and love can live in the same heart at the same time. And I also don't believe love comes to the person who has been offended until he or she forgives the offender. It might take weeks, months, even years. And it may never happen. The hurt is too deep, too hard to overcome, and too raw to find common ground. But until we make peace with the one who has offended us, we'll carry a grudge.

I've done it, so I know. I carried a grudge for twenty-five years toward someone who hurt me deeply, and there was hardly a day I was without the pain of it down deep in my heart. Sometimes it was so deep it was only a little bubble that would pop every now and then reminding me it was still there, and other times it was like a big balloon that got in the way of my breathing; but I was never without that feeling of resentment toward the one who hurt me.

What did it take for me to learn to love through the pain? Oh my! Where to start? I guess the first thing was I had to get sick enough of it to want that feeling to go away. As I've said before (in the words of my mother), "We don't change until we get sick of ourselves." For years, I somehow "enjoyed" carrying a grudge. I felt justified, so I spent my time wishing ill will on my offender. I played with thoughts about it in my mind, going through a labyrinth of bad things I wanted to happen to her. She deserved to suffer. She deserved no forgiveness. She deserved to be without my friendship (as if it mattered to her in the first place!).

But I finally began to get sick and tired of the feeling and decided to talk to God about it. I wanted to change but didn't believe I could do it without help. Ralph Waldo Emerson once said, "Our chief want in life is somebody who shall make us do what we can," and I knew God would be the only One who could prompt me into that.

I confessed how I felt—often with lots of tears and heartache. I literally poured out my agony on Him, and He took it. I could *feel* that He took it because my hatred toward this person began to lift. That's when I realized God was doing something miraculous inside.

Once I started feeling that, I literally gave the whole thing to God to take off my shoulders. And He did it! Then I asked Him to show me what to do next. In His caring, supernatural way, He gave me creative ideas of how to contact this person and try to find a point of reconciliation and balance between us. It was one of the hardest things I ever did. Remember, twenty-five years had passed since the offense. The irony was that when I contacted her, she never brought it up, and neither did I. But somehow we experienced a feeling of commonality and love. Almost. Not quite love . . . but getting there. And I was beginning to feel forgiveness toward her in my heart.

I made efforts to see her, communicated with her, wrote her (she lived in another city and state), and finally I realized there was no more animosity or hatred toward her in any way. Love was back, and the pain was gone. In fact, our relationship was sweeter and richer the second time around.

Love As Jesus Loves

Let me try to list the steps of how this happens so you can use these ideas in your own life as need be:

First, *work out in your own mind exactly what's wrong.* Identify the problem; call it what it is and take it apart piece by piece. Admit where you were wrong and where the other person was wrong. You might write all this down in your private journal. This is all just between you and your very hurt ego!

Second, *start talking to God about it.* (This would probably be best to be number one, but in my case it didn't work that way. I had to analyze it first and take it apart until I felt I could make sense of it when I talked to God. But that's just me). Be very, very honest with what hurts and why. Stay at this task until you feel God's direction on how to change things.

Third, *be brave and courageous*. Contact the offender in your calmest manner and trust God to help you find creative ways to make things right . . . unless you want to go to your grave carrying this feeling of hatred and heartache.

Finally, *don't back down from your commitment to get rid of the feelings of hurt and pain*. Love with all your heart, and never stop loving. Find scriptures to support your quest, and believe you will get better. And . . . you will.

> Have you come to the Red Sea place in your life,
> Where, in spite of all you can do,
> There is no way out, there is no way back,
>> There is no way but through?[1]

Our entire purpose in life is to learn to love as Jesus loves. And how does He love? Unselfishly, constantly, deeply, purely, generously. As long as we are in the human condition, this will not be easy. Count on it. There will be people who will get under our skin so badly we'll want to throttle them, but trust me on this—it *is* possible to love them. Sometimes the difficulty of loving comes in the tiniest ways—when people are petty or aggravating or they interrupt your day or they want more of you than you want to give. That kind of behavior is a pain in the neck. But we're commanded to love these people. The only way we can do it is to ask God for patience and kindness and then to believe He gives it to us in order to reach out to others with those two attributes under our belt.

It's the Golden Rule in Block Letters and Neon Lights!

There are also times we bring pain on ourselves. We've been treated unfairly by "the system." Somebody gets a promotion, and we don't. Somebody gets selected for a team, and we don't. Somebody gets to go with the cute guy, and we don't. What then? How do we handle those crazy-making dilemmas?

For me . . . I talk to myself first. I tell myself it's not fair and I don't like it. (I'm a big fan of "fair." I hate things that aren't fair or equal. But, if I'm honest, I have to admit that life itself isn't fair; and as long as I'm in this life, it ain't ever gonna be fair. *So face that first, Lucille, and move on.*) I do my best to get beyond it. And getting beyond something takes commitment. I think it also takes wanting to be an adult. Wanting maturity. God's going to do His best to bring us all to maturity, but we can help a bit by shutting up and getting out of His way.

I've come to realize that loving through pain is one of

life's greatest teachers with the lowest salary. There's no amount of money that could pay for the lessons learned while I was in agony, and there's no amount I would take in place of the learning. They've taught me to be careful and prayerful and to thank God for His lessons every day.

Joy to forgive and joy to be forgiven
Hang level in the balances of love.[2]

15 *Love: How it Works*

As a shareholder with Starbucks coffee, I always receive their annual reports. I love those little booklets, because there's invariably a card attached inside that offers me a three-dollar cup of coffee, free! This year, it was one of their plastic credit cards with a photo of green grapes on it and a line of type indicating I'm a shareholder. I'm saving that thing forever, reloading it and using it.

Since I love Starbucks, and all my close friends love Starbucks (my favorite is a decaf mocha frappachino with dollop of whipped cream), I plan to keep my plastic card filled with a chunk o' change so I can run down there at a moment's notice and splurge. I look at this card as a kind of personal status symbol in the Starbucks chain of command. Even being at the bottom of the totem pole means a lot to me. I'm part of the clan.

In addition to the credit card coming in the report this year, there was also something else. Something better—their motto. It was in big red letters, printed right on front of the booklet. It said this:

The Humble Coffee Tree

Not only integral to our success as a Company, it also serves as a wonderful example for us to follow.

Draw from your roots. (Trust in and nurture the strength of your core).

Always reach upward.

Always reach out.

And perhaps most important, always give back.

When I read that, I thought, *That's exactly what I want to do in my life—have a strong root system, reach up to the Lord, reach out to others, and give back what I've been given.* I want to be like a tree—a sturdy, dependable person who stands strong during the storms of life and doesn't weaken when the winds blow or trouble rains down on me.

Isaiah 61:3 calls these strong people "oaks of righteousness." They announce freedom to those in bondage.

Jeremiah 17:7–8 says, "Blessed is the man who trusts me, GOD, the woman who sticks with GOD. They're like trees replanted in Eden, putting down roots near the rivers— Never a worry through the hottest of summers, never dropping a leaf, serene and calm through droughts, bearing fresh fruit every season" (MSG).

Trying to reach this goal is a worthy pursuit, but it's not an easy one. To draw strength from one's roots, stretch out to God, reach out to others, and give back in proportion to what we've been given is a 24/7 task. How do we even start that long obedience in the proper direction?

Now that I'm in my seventies, I often think about life itself . . . not just the dailiness of it, but the whole of it . . . the big, round ball of it rolled into one. I ask myself questions. I answer myself. I ask God questions. I listen for His answers. I wait. I wonder. I ponder. I reflect. I project into the future. I dream and contemplate and meditate . . . probably more than I act.

I'm at the age where thought processes and quiet behavior patterns are more prevalent. In my twenties, thirties, forties, and even my fifties, I was completely active. But as I began my sixties and now seventies, I spend more time thinking back on what brought me here than trying to *get here*. I'm here now.

I'm not saying, "I've arrived," in the sense one brags on

having reached the pinnacle of her lifelong dream, but I now know the difference between folly and wisdom. In the words of the British poet William Blake, "A fool sees not the same tree that a wise man sees." I look at things differently than I did in my youth when I lacked experience, judgment, and prudence.

I reread some of the underlinings in the books I devoured forty or fifty years ago and try to contemplate what I felt when I underlined that. Have I changed since then? If so, how? If not, why? What does it take to grow up . . . to reach maturity?

To answer these questions, I have to look back and answer some of the questions that are most frequently asked of me.

What Were Your Parents Like?

My father was fifteen years older than my mother. He had been divorced before and had a son by his first marriage. He was a tall, handsome, kind, tender man who felt deeply and cried easily and was utterly devoted to my mother. He was a disciplinarian but in an understanding way. Before he spanked us as children, he explained the principle of why he was doing so. I wanted him to forget the principle and get on with the spanking just to get it over with, but he wanted to explain everything.

Daddy had a very dedicated work ethic and felt strongly about his children being all they could be on the job. Show up early! Work overtime! Never ask for a raise! All that and more. He was a believer in Jesus Christ and loved God's Word. He used to quote Bible verses to me to encourage me and never wrote me a letter without it having at least five or six Scripture references.

Daddy didn't have a college degree, but he encouraged my brothers and me to get all the schooling we could. He wasn't adamant about college but was proud of us when we came home with academic achievements. He loved to laugh and have a good time and was a bit of a practical joker. He was my hero all my life and was the most wonderful man who ever lived, in my opinion. He died at the age of eighty-seven in 1980, having suffered a stroke in church one Sunday about three years before when my brother Chuck was preaching. Daddy never fully recovered from that, and gradually, month after month, went downhill until his death.

My mother was quite different from Daddy. She was twenty-three when they married, having quit college in order to marry him. They fell in love in the late 1920s and were married in 1930. Mother was artistic, musical, domestic, funny, and, unfortunately, very moody. While my dad was laid back and passive, Mother was quite the opposite. She was high control but not a disciplinarian. She left that up to Daddy. Mother loved people and was energized by them. Daddy was just the opposite; he just wanted to be with his family. That was enough for him, and he felt complete and totally happy when his wife and children surrounded him.

Mother was the soul of hospitality, and nobody gave a dinner party that was more fun than hers. She loved to laugh and found humor in everyday life.

Together, Mother and Daddy were the perfect example that opposites attract. But they were devoted to each other, never argued (to my knowledge), supported what their children did, and were eager for us to be "civilized." My best gift from them was their utter love and dedication to God's calling as parents. They were exemplary in that regard.

How Have You Made Single Life Work So Well for You?

The primary reason being single has worked well for me is that I've never wanted to be married. It's never been an issue I had to work through. As a child, I had many dreams

I wanted to see come true—travel all over the world, sing professionally, get a college education, and have a career. I never thought marriage could bring me the fulfillment that the realization of these dreams could. It never occurred to me I couldn't fulfill my dreams, because I was so verbally and emotionally supported by my father. He told me I could do anything I wanted to and go anywhere in the world . . . and I believed him. He was my cheerleader from my youngest years.

Though single, I've always had a lot of people in my life. However, there's a side of me that's very much a loner. Although there are times I love being surrounded by people, I also enjoy solitude. My friends aren't my source of energy like they were my mother's, but there have always been a few people in whom I confide and with whom I share my deepest hurts and sorrows. These persons are always those of like faith and motive and from whom I receive love, support, and encouragement. They are lifelong friends.

I learned a long time ago that single life is not easy. But neither is being married; because life is profoundly disappointing, remember? I truly believe life is what we make it, and my temperament is such that I look for the fun in life and seek out friends that aren't negative. This makes a huge difference in how one faces problems.

What Is Your Formula to Maintaining Rich, Meaningful Relationships?

First of all, there's no formula, because every relationship is different from another. But for me there are two major qualifiers to having friends and being a good friend to somebody else.

First, I hold people loosely in my heart. I used to be very hurt when people didn't do things my way or when they chose to be with somebody else. I felt left out and went into a horrible funk. I pouted. I was rude and indifferent to the one who hurt me. Very childish! But when I got sick enough of acting that way, I brought God into the problem and asked Him to help me grow up. When your heart is broken, you either die there or you start growing up. You stop being petty and petulant. You release your will and your grip on those who really mean something to you. There's nothing like being free, and that's one of the main ingredients in a meaningful friendship—to be free and let the other person be free.

Second, a rich relationship has to have an investment from both persons. It's like a bank account—if you want it to grow, you keep making deposits. Sometimes you have to transfer money from one account to another to balance your financial picture. It's the same principle with relationships. Friendships don't grow rich unless you make deposits: you spend time together, you connect with each other, and you change things around to give balance where it's needed. You constantly have to study the input of that account to see what it needs. I promise you, if you take care of the relationship, it will grow.

Here are a few attributes that need to be present and fostered or the relationship will have trouble—forgiveness, patience, mutuality, and thoughtfulness. Also, I can't say enough about the fine art of listening. Marilyn Meberg has mastered that art. She has no peer. Teach yourself to wait until the other person stops speaking before you speak. Try your best not to butt in. And own up to it if a disagreement is your fault.

How Did You Get So Organized, and What Keeps You That Way?

Being organized is a habit. In great part, I was probably born this way. It's in my DNA. My father was very organized, and I admired that. Why? Because he could put his hands on anything at any given moment. Everything had a place, and everything was in its place.

I don't think clearly unless my surroundings are neat. Messes make me muddled in my brain, and I don't like that feeling. Being neat works well for me because it enables me to produce, and I love the sense of accomplishment. (You have to realize most of this is possible because I live alone. If I didn't, this would probably never work.)

Another reason I enjoy organization is that I love stuff. I have so much of it, and if I let it get out of hand for very long, I'd be buried in my own home. So I go through little rituals to keep things organized. I say to myself, "OK, Luci . . . handle papers one time only; look for shortcuts, and if there isn't one, don't try to make one; be patient with yourself; don't make snap decisions; have a place for everything, and return what you use to that place."

I also write everything down. I keep lists. I love lists! I journal and have for years and years. I carry little books, jotters, and small binders everywhere. I go back and read what I've written and try to understand principles and patterns that are emerging . . . and then I use those as a guide to the future.

Why Is Your Life So Full of Joy?

My life is not full of joy every minute, but it's true that joy is my most natural posture. I had a happy childhood, and that no doubt makes a big difference in the way I am today.

In addition, I've trained myself to look for the bright side of things. I'm rarely around negative people, and if I am, I don't make camp there.

Joy is not only a marvelous gift from God; it's a command (Philippians 4:4 says, "Rejoice!"). Joy is also a learned behavior. If you're generous with other people, they will be generous with you, and that alone will bring you unspeakable joy. Joy starts inside yourself. You can't expect to get it from somebody else first.

Although I experience abundant joy in life, laugh heartily and often, and appreciate humor at every turn, my temperament poses certain challenges: When I tire, I get cranky. When things are out of order, I can be stubbornly controlling. When I find myself at the mercy of another's plans or schedule, I can be very frustrated. In that sense, joy does not always come naturally to me . . . it's an attitude I choose and try very hard to maintain.

Do You Ever Struggle with Fear or Doubt?

I would say rarely. By nature, I'm not prone to fear. I really, really, really try to believe what God says and trust Him to come through with the goods. When He says I don't have to be afraid, I try hard to believe that and go on. When He says He will always be with me, I know He will. When He promises to provide for my needs, I look to Him to do that. When He listens when I talk to Him, it makes me want to spend time doing that. In short . . . when I take God at His word, I don't have many doubts or fears.

The key to all this is learning to trust God in every little nook and cranny of your day. Life works when we trust, and the love comes because we feel blessed in that trust. We love the One who keeps His word.

I encourage you to go through life thinking about what you're doing. Don't just treat what comes your way as one more thing to go through. There's a purpose in everything that happens. Ask yourself, "What could God be teaching me in this?" Try to answer that question as honestly as you can.

Commit your way to the Lord, and see where He takes you. Remember, even when you are struggling, He is not making a mistake with your life.

Life! Celebrate It

16 *Love Who You Are*

Perhaps the poet and playwright e. e. cummings said it best: "To be nobody but yourself in a world which is doing its best, night and day, to make you everybody else—means to fight the hardest battle which any human being can fight; and never stop fighting."

Would everybody who loves yourself please raise your hand? Not many hands going up, are there? To love oneself was sort of frowned on when I was young. At least, it wasn't encouraged in Christian circles where I grew up. If the truth were known, we didn't talk about it much. Because conceit, pride, and arrogance were frowned upon, I suppose I equated them with loving yourself. We were taught to put others first, to give place to those around us, and to take a backseat when others were present.

I've lived a long time since then and have had lots of opportunity to rethink this concept of loving who you are. I view it somewhat differently now. I still know conceit, pride, and arrogance are wrong, and I still believe in a servant spirit—more than ever—but I've learned that loving one's self is actually a biblical command. It's stated in an interesting way, so it's often misunderstood—but it's there.

In the book of Matthew, Jesus says, "Love your neighbor as yourself" (19:19; 22:39). And Paul says in Galatians 5:14 that the law is fulfilled when you "love your neighbor as yourself." Again, Romans 13:9 and James 2:8 reiterates the command to love your neighbor as yourself. In every case, loving your neighbor is predicated on loving yourself first. What does that mean?

There are many verses that tell us how to treat a neighbor. Among God's commands are don't lie to your neighbor (Exodus 20:16); don't defraud your neighbor (Leviticus 19:13); stand up for your neighbor (Job 16:21); don't betray confidences told to you by your neighbor (Proverbs 25:9). But my favorite is the consummate verse about loving one's neighbor, Romans 13:10: "Love other people as well as you do yourself. You can't go wrong when you love others. When you add up everything in the law code, the sum total is love" (MSG). Basically, loving ourselves is defined by the same standard by which we love others.

When e. e. cummings said it's hard to be ourselves, I think he could have just as strongly said it's almost impossible to love ourselves. So often we don't like who we are. We don't like what we see in the mirror, we're dissatisfied with how we look or what we weigh, or we're disappointed in how we've misbehaved or how we've treated someone else. And the sum total of that prevents us from truly loving ourselves.

At one time or another I've felt unlovable for all the reasons listed above, and I imagine you have too. And on rare occasions, I still do. But I've learned that God loves me, no matter what. As long as I am confident in God's love for me, I eventually come around to the realization I can love me too.

What happens when I love me unconditionally? Well, I'm more content, I feel appreciated, I'm sweeter to other people, I don't get my feelings hurt because I'm secure inside, and I do things for other people without expecting something from them in return—all those things and more. In short, I do unto others what I want done unto me!

Let me give you an example. I had a gathering at my house for several of my neighbors recently. It was actually in honor of the president of Thomas Nelson, Inc.—Mike

Hyatt and his wife, Gail. (Thomas Nelson is the parent company of Women of Faith.) Because I'm crazy about this couple, I decided to distinguish them in a special way by giving a seated dinner party and inviting the neighbors closest to my heart, all of whom live within a two- or three-mile radius. This included my brother Chuck and his wife Cynthia, Barry and Sheila Walsh, Nicole Johnson, Marilyn Meberg, Mary Graham, and Ney Bailey. Most of us work for Women of Faith, but not all. In total, there were ten people on the guest list and me, their hostess.

I worked on this party for weeks, and it was such a delight to plan and execute because I love all these people so much. I invited everyone a month or so in advance and set my long table in the dining room/library with my best tablecloth and napkins, fine china, silver, and crystal. I made place cards, ordered fresh flowers, and arranged my iPod background music exactly in the order I wanted it played throughout the evening. I had the meal catered, with two servers taking care of things so all the guests could completely relax, have fun, tell stories, and not have to lift a finger to help.

We had prayer before the meal, and for four and a half hours, we enjoyed the fellowship and fun of an evening together with friends. Laughter filled the air. We talked about movies, books, families, travel . . . things we all love to discuss, and the time just flew. It went way too fast and before we knew it, the evening was over.

Was I sorry I had done all that work for something that lasted only a few hours? Absolutely not. Did I spend too much money to make everything just right? Not on your life. Did I regret going to all that trouble? Absolutely not. I did it because I love these people. They're my neighbors in the real sense as well as the biblical sense. And they're my dearest friends.

But I would have done it had I not had fine china, fresh flowers, a catered meal, or paid servants to wait on us . . . as I have done so many times. I used to host dinner parties with friends when I had little or no money because it's not about money. It's about love!

I've also done it for *just me*. Since I'm not married and live alone, it's up to me to create a life of love and beauty, joy and fun. I do it for me. I don't wait for somebody else to fill a gap in my life. Christ has filled that gap, and I've learned to be content when I'm alone and define myself by Christ alone—with nobody else in that definition.

I love parties of all kinds. And I love going to dinner at the home of other people. I enjoy it if it's formal or casual; for two hundred or two; with a catered meal or hamburgers. What matters is not what we have but how much we love each other.

Getting on God's Guest List

A few months ago, I was reading Psalms in *The Message* and discovered (as if for the first time) Psalm 15. It's fantastic. Short. Powerful. And so apropos to what I'm saying in this chapter. Listen to the opening thought: "GOD, who gets invited to dinner at your place? How do we get on your guest list?" (v. 1).

Aren't those great questions? We all want to know the answer because we all want to sit at God's dining table. We long to have fellowship and fun with Him. We want to see how He sets the table and who else is there and find out what will be the topics of conversation. And here's the great part—he tells us in the next few verses what it takes to get on that list. He says, "Walk straight, act right, tell the truth. Don't hurt your friend, don't blame your neighbor; despise the despicable. Keep your word even when it costs you, make an honest living, never take a bribe" (vv. 2–5).

That list is perfect, because there's not one thing there about how the person has to be dressed or what he must weigh, or whether he has money or is educated or famous. There's nothing about looks or beauty or ability. It's all—*all!*—about character. It's about the inside of the person. And who doesn't want to be with people like that? This is what we want in a dinner guest. It's what we want in a friend. It's what we want in a neighbor. It's what we want in ourselves.

The psalm closes with this final verse: "You'll never get blacklisted if you live like this" (v. 5). That means you'll be invited to every dinner party in town. It's what God requires in order to be on His guest list, and you can bet your bottom dollar that if you value these attributes as well, you'll be right at the top of everybody's list.

Learn to Accept Yourself As You Are

This chapter is about loving who you are—about accepting yourself as you are and not going through life trying to fake it because you wish you were somebody else. It's putting stock in character instead of playing charades. No one I know is able to maintain these behavior patterns all the time. The apostle Paul was right when he said that which we don't want to do we find ourselves doing and that which we want to do, we so often don't (see Romans 7:19). That's why being yourself is "the hardest battle that any human being can fight and never stop fighting."

Let me suggest ten areas I work on when I get bogged down and forget to love myself as God commanded me to. Nobody has a corner on these things, and you already know every one of them by heart. But when you forget, these are reminders:

- Be content with what you have.
- Stop comparing.
- Count your blessings.
- Quit personalizing every comment.
- Maintain a servant spirit.
- Do the unexpected for a loved one.
- Keep a heart of gratitude.
- Don't be negative.
- Respect yourself.
- Take God at His word.

Sometimes, no matter what we do or how hard we try to remember these suggestions, we still feel completely unloved. Unloved by ourselves, unloved by others, and definitely unloved by God. We feel nobody sees or knows or understands or cares about us. This is part of the madness of being in the human condition. We simply feel invisible. We want to scream or cry or misbehave to make our presence known. We want attention. So we conjure up actions that are totally contrary to who we really are in order to be visible. My friend Nicole Johnson has said,

"Invisibility is not inflicted upon me; it is a gift to help me truly serve." Well put, Nikki!

Many years ago, a dear friend sent me a poetry book, and in it he marked a poem that reminded him of me, he said. The poet, Alexander Pope, calls it "The Quiet Life." I've read it often and feel it does, in a way, capture my essence. I can't identify with every line, but I most definitely identify with its message. In closing, I'll share it with you:

Happy the man, whose wish and care
    A few paternal acres bound,
Content to breathe his native air in his own ground.

Whose herds with milk, whose fields with bread,
    Whose flocks supply him with attire;
Whose trees in summer yield him shade, in winter fire.

Blest, who can unconcern'dly find
    Hours, days, and years slide soft away
In health of body, peace of mind, quiet by day,

Sound sleep by night; study and ease
    Together mix'd; sweet recreation,
And innocence, which most does please with meditation.

Thus let me live, unseen, unknown;

    Thus unlamented let me die;

Steal from the world, and not a stone tell where I lie.[1]

Forward

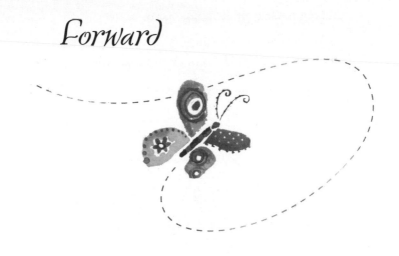

Just one last word before we part!

I hope this book has been an encouragement to you. As I've shared my thoughts, ideas, stories, and lessons learned, I have done so with the desire to help you become more of who you are, not to ask you to be like me. Each of us is rich within ourselves. God has given us great capacity to grow and change . . . often exceeding our own expectations . . . in order to become all we can be by His grace.

Please follow your own instincts as you go forward. If you're a believer in Jesus Christ, you have the Holy Spirit inside to be your guide. As you become mature through knowledge of God's Word, He will open doors for you to be an encouragement to others. In fact, He'll reach out to others *through* you. Count on it! Second Corinthians 1:5 describes this process of being encouraged to be encouraging to others: "He comes alongside us when we go through hard times, and before you know it, He brings us alongside someone else who is going through hard times so that we can be there for that person just as God was there for us" (MSG).

It's a responsibility and privilege to be yourself, and not someone else. Remember in the very beginning of this book I talked about each of us being on a full sea of possibilities and opportunities? Well, that's where we are . . . out in the boat heading toward the future with God as our Captain.

Let your hook be always cast; in the pool where you least expect it, there will be a fish.

—Ovid

Notes

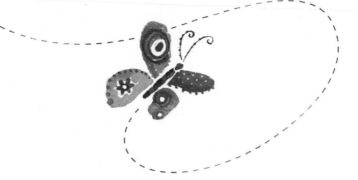

Backward

1. Louise van Swaaji and Jean Klare, *The Atlas of Experience* (London: Bloomsbury, 2000)

Chapter 2—Listen with Your Heart

1. To read more about Alexandra Scott or to purchase products to benefit pediatric cancer research, visit www.alexslemonade.com.
2. Millard Fuller, *Love in the Mortar Joints: The Story of Habitat for Humanity* (El Monte, Calif.: New Win, 1980).
3. For more information about Habitat for Humanity International, see www.habitat.org.

Chapter 6—Learn What to Spend

1. Sara Teasdale, *The Collected Poems of Sara Teasdale* (New York: The MacMillan Company,1968), 97.

Chapter 8—Learn When to Stop

1. From *At Seventy* by May Sarton. Copyright © 1984 by May Sarton. Used by permission of W. W. Norton & Company, Inc.
2. Sarah and A. Elizabeth Delaney with Amy Hill Hearth, *Having Our Say: The Delany Sisters' First 100 Years* (New York: Dell, 1993).

Chapter 13—Love What You're Doing

1. Larry Crabb, *Inside Out* (Colorado Springs: NavPress, 1988).
2. Ibid.

Chapter 14—Love Though It's Painful

1. Annie Johnson Flint, quoted in John Bartlett, *Familiar Quotations* (Boston: Little, Brown and Company, 1951), 763.
2. Richard Garnett, quoted in John Bartlett, *Familiar Quotations* (Boston: Little, Brown and Company, 1951), 617.

Chapter 16—Love Who You Are

1. Alexander Pope, "The Quiet Life," quoted in Francis Turner Palgrave, *The Golden Treasury of the Best Songs and Lyrical Poems in the English Language* (London: Collins, 1963), 136.

Other Selections for Women of Faith

Best-Selling authors and Women of Faith® speakers Patsy Clairmont, Mary Graham, Barbara Johnson, Marilyn Meberg, Grammy Award Winning singer Sandi Patty, Luci Swindoll, Sheila Walsh, Thelma Wells and dramatist Nicole Johnson bring humor and insight to women's daily lives. Sit back, exhale, and enjoy spending some time with these extraordinary women!

WOMEN OF FAITH®

Contagious JOY 2006

2006 EVENT CITIES & SPECIAL GUESTS

FEBRUARY 23-25
NATIONAL
FT. LAUDERDALE, FL
BankAtlantic Center

MARCH 31-APRIL 1
SHREVEPORT, LA
CenturyTel Center
Avalon, Kathy Troccoli,
Anita Renfroe,
Donna VanLiere

APRIL 7-8
HOUSTON, TX
Toyota Center
Avalon, Max Lucado,
Chonda Pierce,
Donna VanLiere

APRIL 21-22
SPOKANE, WA
Spokane Arena
Avalon, Natalie Grant,
Anita Renfroe

APRIL 28-29
COLUMBUS, OH
Nationwide Arena
Natalie Grant,
Anita Renfroe,
Jennifer Rothschild

JUNE 2-3
OMAHA, NE
Qwest Center
Avalon, Anita Renfroe,
Tammy Trent,
Donna VanLiere

JUNE 9-10
ROCHESTER, NY
Blue Cross Arena
Avalon, Kathy Troccoli,
CeCe Winans,
Donna VanLiere

JUNE 16-17
FRESNO, CA
SaveMart Center*
Avalon, Natalie Grant,
Max Lucado,
Donna VanLiere

JUNE 23-24
ATLANTA, GA
Philips Arena
Avalon,
Nichole Nordeman,
Sherri Shepherd,
Donna VanLiere

JULY 7-8
CHICAGO, IL
United Center
Avalon,
Anita Renfroe,
CeCe Winans

JULY 14-15
CLEVELAND, OH
Quicken Loans Arena
Avalon, Natalie Grant,
Sherri Shepherd

JULY 21-22
WASHINGTON, DC
MCI Center
Avalon, Chonda Pierce,
Sherri Shepherd

JULY 28-29
CALGARY, ALBERTA
Pengrowth Saddledome*
Avalon, Carried Away,
Max Lucado,
Donna VanLiere

AUGUST 4-5
ST. LOUIS, MO
Savvis Center
Natalie Grant,
Anita Renfroe,
Sherri Shepherd,
Donna VanLiere

AUGUST 11-12
HARTFORD, CT
Hartford Civic Center
Avalon, Carol Kent,
Jennifer Rothschild

AUGUST 18-19
FT. WAYNE, IN
War Memorial Coliseum
Avalon, Natalie Grant,
Carol Kent

AUGUST 25-26
DALLAS, TX
American Airlines Center
Max Lucado,
Natalie Grant,
Robin McGraw

SEPTEMBER 8-9
ANAHEIM, CA
Arrowhead Pond
Avalon, Robin McGraw,
Jennifer Rothschild

SEPTEMBER 15-16
PHILADELPHIA, PA
Wachovia Center
Avalon, Robin McGraw,
Nicole C. Mullen

SEPTEMBER 22-23
DENVER, CO
Pepsi Center
Max Lucado,
Chonda Pierce,
Kathy Troccoli

SEPTEMBER 29-30
SACRAMENTO, CA
ARCO Arena
Avalon, Robin McGraw,
Nichole Nordeman

OCTOBER 6-7
OKLAHOMA CITY, OK
Ford Center
Avalon, Max Lucado,
Jennifer Rothschild,
Donna VanLiere

OCTOBER 13-14
PORTLAND, OR
Rose Garden Arena
Avalon, Carol Kent,
Kathy Troccoli,
Donna VanLiere

OCTOBER 20-21
ST. PAUL, MN
Xcel Energy Center
Avalon, Carol Kent,
Anita Renfroe

OCTOBER 27-28
CHARLOTTE, NC
Charlotte Arena
Avalon, Chonda Pierce,
Jennifer Rothschild

NOVEMBER 3-4
VANCOUVER, BC
GM Place*
Avalon, Carried Away,
Nichole Nordeman,
Donna VanLiere

NOVEMBER 10-11
ORLANDO, FL
TD Waterhouse C
Avalon,
Nicole C. M
Anita Ren
Donna V

NOVE
PH
Gl

1-888-49-FAITH womenoffaith.

*No Pre-Conference available. Dates, times, locations and special guests subj
Visit womenoffaith.com for details on special guests, registration deadlines